SOCIAL SKILLS & COMMUNICATION MASTERY (2 IN 1)

CONQUER CONVERSATIONS & UPGRADE YOUR CHARISMA. LEARN HOW TO ANALYZE PEOPLE, OVERCOME SHYNESS & BOOST YOUR EMOTIONAL INTELLIGENCE (EQ)

STEWART HUNTER

DEVON HOUSE
PRESS

CONTENTS

Part III

KEEPING YOUR RELATIONSHIPS AND
MAKING THEM LAST

INTRODUCTION

You're in a room with several other people who are idly chatting away. You desperately want to be part of the conversation, but you find yourself frozen to the spot, unable to think of a single witty thing to say. Fear starts to creep up your spine, feeling cast out, lost, and completely inept.

Does this sound familiar?

More people struggle with socializing than you might realize. When it's happening to you, it feels like you're the only one in the world who feels that way, but in reality, it's not true. Many of the people chatting away in the room, seeming completely at ease, actually find it hard to open up and socialize with other people. The difference between you and them? They've learned the tools to completely hide their fear and show confidence in its place. They know how to respond to other people and read their body language. They get exactly what they need to do in order to make themselves feel as comfortable as possible.

You can be that person seeming at ease in a crowd. You don't know it yet, but you can.

I understand how you feel right now. You want to build relationships with those around you, you want to be able to talk and feel at ease, you don't want to worry about what people are going to think when you speak your mind, and you want to hold a conversation without always being on edge. You would love to be able to go to a party and not worry for hours beforehand about making small talk. You desperately want to build up your social circle, but the starting point of having to actually speak to people you don't know leaves you paralyzed with fear.

I understand you and I sympathize with you. However, the fact you're reading this book is the first brave step towards improving your social skills and kicking shyness and bad communication habits out of your life for good. So, pat yourself on the back for that!

You need to understand what you're doing wrong, you need to identify those bad habits and eradicate them, replacing them with good habits, and you need to learn the tools and skills to help you socialize in an easier and more free-flowing manner.

That's where this book comes in.

WHY SHOULD YOU TRUST A WORD I SAY?

You're probably reading this, rolling your eyes and wondering who on Earth I am and why I'm the authority on socializing. Well, let me tell you my story.

The reason I understand how you're feeling is that I've been where you are now. I was a shy child, and this didn't seem to change as I moved into my adolescence and early 20s. Whilst my friends at school were motoring their way through their first experiences, meeting new people, having their first relationships, going out for the first time, dreaming about what they were going to do with their career, and actually doing something about it rather than just dreaming, I was static. I had dreams, believe me, I had plenty, but acting upon them was far too much for me. I had friends, but I was always the quiet one, the one everyone thought was a little strange because I didn't say much. I blushed more than I wanted to, and I found myself stuttering over my words whenever I was put on the spot.

I berated myself every single night as I laid in bed for all the bumbling I did throughout the day. In my head, I was a confident person, I was happy, full of life, and easy in social situations. In reality, everything was the opposite. The worst thing was that I knew what I wanted to say, I could hold all of these conversations in my head and have them with ease.

You see, shyness isn't introversion. You can be introverted and not at all shy. Shyness is something else altogether. Shyness leaves you paralyzed when surrounded by people. You tell yourself that whatever you say won't be good enough, that people will laugh, or that your voice will come out all squeaky and you'll embarrass yourself. It's a fear of social situations but let me tell you something – fears can be overcome.

I overcame my shyness. How? Through hard work and focus. I had to face my fears, I had to push through those walls I'd built up around me. It was hard, it was scary at times, but it's the biggest achievement of my life to date. I worked out what I was doing wrong and I learned new habits to replace them. These days, socializing doesn't fill me with dread. I'll probably never be the world's most natural conversationalist, but I no longer worry about it, and I'm able to have easy conversations with those around me. I've met new friends because of it, I've had new relationships, and I've built up my career.

You can do all of this too.

I want to help you to achieve the same thing. I want to share what I learned and the techniques that worked for me. Then, I want you to share all of that with other people in your life who might be struggling.

The saddest part of all of this is that there are millions of people walking around, struggling with their social skills. It's holding them back; it's stopping them from living their best lives. It's stopping them from forming close relationships with other people. But, it can all be changed – the issue is that most people don't know that they can change their situation, so they simply carry on in the same way.

That's not going to be your fate.

This book will change your life. That's a bold statement, I know, but it's a true one. Being more confident in your ability to socialize will open so many doors for you, both in your professional and personal lives. You'll build those close relationships that have eluded you so far, and your fear of socializing will slowly ebb away.

Can you imagine how good that will feel?

Countless people in the world have overcome their shyness and poor social skills, creating a new life for themselves. You only have to do a quick Google search to find a whole range of such people, and they followed exactly the same advice that you're going to read in this book.

MY PROMISE TO YOU

By the end of this book, I promise that you'll be able to not only feel more confident in your future ability, but you'll be able to identify the problems that have been holding you back and overcome them. From that, you'll start to try out your new skills and you'll see the results coming your way, showing you that the progress you've made was more than worth the results.

Put simply, you will conquer your problems and you'll master socializing as a result.

So, why hang around for a second longer?

Your shyness has held you back long enough. Do not give it another second of your time or attention. Now, turn your focus towards the strategies and advice in this book, implementing them into your daily routine and looking forward to the results.

The alternative? Of course, you could simply continue as you are. You could assume that it's just too hard or that it's not going to work for you. As a result, you'll continue struggling to communicate, you'll always find it hard to build relationships with people, and you'll always be socially inept.

Is that what you want for yourself? Do you want to continue missing opportunities and watching them pass you by?

Of course, you don't, and that's why if you're smart (and I know you are), you'll turn the page and begin your journey.

I

TAKING THE FIRST STEPS: BEING AWARE OF YOURSELF

WHAT YOU NEED TO KNOW ABOUT EMOTIONAL INTELLIGENCE

You've made it to the first chapter, so give yourself a pat on the back. That means you've shown a willingness to start making changes in your life and begin the first step on your journey.

Whenever you want to change something in your life, you first need to acknowledge the problem. That's often the hardest part. It means admitting that something in your life just isn't working, but that is what will allow you to grow and improve.

This first chapter is going to focus on emotional intelligence, or EQ. This is important because it overlaps with every single part of what you're trying to work towards. You want to be able to socialize better, you want to communicate better, you want to connect with others. Having a higher level of EQ will allow you to do all of those things.

We'll explore what EQ is, why it is different from another very simi-lar-sounding term, IQ, and we're going to go on to talk about the components. I'm then going to help you explore how low your EQ may be, because I'm sorry to say this – the problems you're having indicate low EQ. BUT – there is always a but – this is a fluctuant level which can be increased with some ongoing work.

First things first, let's work out exactly what EQ is.

EMOTIONAL INTELLIGENCE (EQ) - WHAT IS IT & HOW IS IT DIFFERENT FROM IQ?

There are two terms that are very often confused – EQ and IQ. This book is going to focus on EQ, because as someone who struggles in social situations and with communication generally, your EQ is low.

Now, before you panic, this doesn't mean that you're not intelligent. IQ is a measure of intelligence, EQ is not. EQ stands for emotional intelligence. It's entirely possible for you to have an extremely high IQ, to be an extremely smart person, yet to struggle to communicate with others and connecting, and as a result, your EQ is low.

Let's simplify this thing. EQ isn't about your smarts, it's about:

- How you recognize the emotions in other people
- How you connect with others
- How you communicate with others
- How you understand and manage your own range of emotions
- How you respond to stressful situations and challenges
- How you show empathy to other people
- How you handle conflict.

Emotional intelligence encompasses all of these things but it's far harder to measure than IQ. If you want to know what your IQ is, you can easily do a few cognitive tests and you'll get a pretty good idea of where you're at. With EQ, getting an actual reading is borderline impossible, instead, you need a gauge.

As someone who struggles with communication, socializing, and someone who finds it hard to build relationships with other people because of all of this, your EQ needs a little work. The good news is that working on your EQ will allow you to solve all of the socializing and communication problems that have held you back so far, but it will also help you to manage your own emotions and how you respond to stress and upsets too. You'll become more mindful, you'll be able to live in the moment rather than worrying about the past or future, and as a result, you will be much happier.

Is IQ more important than EQ? Not at all. You can be smart, but you can also be lonely. You can be the cleverest person to ever walk the earth, to be smashing tests left, right, and center, but what use is any of that if you don't have relationships with other people? If you can't speak to others and build friendships? If you can't share it all with the people in your life? For that reason, you could argue, and many people agree, that EQ is far more important in life than IQ could ever be.

WHAT IT MEANS TO HAVE HIGH EQ

So, what does it mean when you have a high EQ level? Does it mean you're always happy, you never struggle, and that everything is roses? Of course not. Life is difficult for everyone from time to time, but when your EQ is higher, it makes it easier for you to handle problems and you're able to see the more positive side of things, rather than assuming that the glass is always half empty, or always will be.

I've outlined above what EQ is in terms of how it allows you to live your life, but what clear benefits does it bring? What will come your way if you dedicate your time and effort to boosting your EQ level? How will it solve your current problems?

You Will Be Able to Handle Change More Positively

Many people struggle with change. It's no surprise, change is sometimes hard to deal with, but it happens throughout the course of life. If you find yourself often being thrown by change and it causes you to feel worried or even scared, building your EQ will help you with that. You will learn to see change as something positive, as a chance to build something new, and you will respond to it more positively in general, seeing the opportunities it could bring you.

You'll Find it Easier to Communicate and Work with Others

In terms of communication, EQ is vital. This works on many different levels, but being able to read others, empathize, and connect means that you can communicate more effectively. Your confidence grows naturally when your EQ level is higher, which certainly helps when communicating with other people, be it individually or within a group. This also means that if you are working with other people, perhaps in a collaborative session, you'll find it easier to put forth your ideas and listen more effectively to the ideas of others.

Difficult Conversations Will Be Far Easier Too

EQ allows you to read other people and gives you an almost sixth sense of what to say versus what not to say. Again, much of this comes down to confidence and self-awareness, which higher EQ will certainly help with. Whenever you're faced with a difficult conversation, either in your personal life or your professional life, building your EQ will allow you to navigate the potential pitfalls with ease, rather than bumbling, stumbling, and potentially saying the wrong thing.

You Will Recognize and Empathize with Others, Building Relationships

If you're still struggling to understand how EQ will help with communication and socializing, this next point should explain it. When you boost your EQ, you're able to understand what isn't being said. You can read body language, you listen to the words other people are saying but you also listen to what isn't being said, such as non-verbal cues, speed of speech, eye contact, etc. All of this helps you read what they really mean.

You will also notice that your natural empathy level will increase as you recognize the emotions in other people. This allows you to naturally build relationships that are built on trust, understanding, and care – the very best type of relationships!

You Will Live in The Moment

A very pleasant side-effect of higher EQ is mindfulness. You can work towards mindfulness as a route towards increasing your EQ, but it almost comes naturally. This means that you're able to allow things to occur in your life without allowing them to take you over completely. I mentioned the ability to deal with change, but it's more than that. It's about not constantly living in the past, or deeply worrying about the future. You'll live in the moment and have a sense of calm because you know that you can handle whatever life throws at you. It's a very comforting feeling.

You Will Find It Easier to Manage Your Own Emotions

You won't just recognize and read the emotions of others, you'll become more aware of your own. This increased self-awareness helps you to manage your emotions as they ebb and flow, avoiding 'in the heat of the moment' actions and also helping you to deal with problems.

People with higher EQ are better and more effective problem solvers, simply because they don't allow their emotions to get the better of them. That's not to say that they never have strong emotions, it's just that they can recognize them and deal with them far more effectively.

Now can you see why EQ is such an important part of the solution to your original problem?

THE FIVE DIFFERENT COMPONENTS OF EQ

The subject of EQ has long been of interest to researchers and five main categories of EQ have been identified. These are:

- Self-awareness
- Self-regulation
- Motivation
- Empathy
- Social skills

All of these are of great interest to you too, given that you are focused upon shedding shyness, increasing your social skills, and allowing yourself to become a better communicator.

Being more self-aware means that you can recognize your emotions and moods, but you can also read how these might be affecting other people around you. Increasing self-awareness means an ability to take yourself less seriously, to not take mistakes so harshly, and also be more aware of how other people view you.

Self-regulation links into self-awareness because you can't really have one without the other. Self-regulation means that you can control your moods and the actions that might come as a result, whilst also avoiding acting upon impulse. This can loosely be interpreted as emotional maturity, and it's also about how you respond to other people and their moods too. For instance, a person who seems short and off-handed is not necessarily upset with you, but instead, they're angry at something else that's going on in their life. Self-awareness and self-regulation allow you to see this and adjust your response correctly.

Another important element of EQ is motivation, and this is what will push you to keep learning and improving yourself throughout your life. You will see and take opportunities as they come your way, and improving your social skills, will also bring you more opportunities as a result. A person with higher EQ will take the initiative and make something happen, rather than sitting back and waiting for it to fall into their lap. It's also about identifying what drives you in life – is it the materialistic ownership of the fanciest phone, or is it success and achievement in your career or personal life?

The next component is empathy, and this is where communication really comes to the fore. When you have empathy, you're able to read other people and understand their emotions, therefore "walking a mile in their shoes". A person with high EQ understands people and situations far more effectively and it helps them to support those around them. This is a vital part of developing relationships and communicating with others.

Finally, we have social skills.

Earlier I mentioned being able to read body language, speech, listening, non-verbal cues, etc. All of this is vital in communication and socializing. It helps you to develop and maintain relationships, whilst also allowing you to have a certain ease in conversations. Empathy links into this as well, as you can find things you have in common and discuss from there. EQ boosts your communication skills, allowing you to be a good conversationalist, whilst also being a leader whenever necessary. It means you can tailor your approach to the situation you're in, and that will bring you many benefits in all areas of your life.

HOW TO IDENTIFY YOUR LEVEL OF EQ

The most natural next step from reading this chapter is going to be a keenness to learn your own EQ level. As I mentioned earlier, it's not as easy to measure EQ as it is to measure IQ. However, you can get a general idea and there are tests you can take which will allow you to get a sense of how much work you need to do in order to boost your own EQ level over time.

You don't have to take a test full of multiple choice questions to give this answer, you can be more aware of your own actions and how you interact (or how you don't interact) and that will give you a good indicator of your EQ level too. To help you with that, let's identify a few very common signs of low EQ. If you notice these on a regular basis, that's your answer!

- You struggle to communicate with those around you
- You often feel like you've failed if someone criticizes you or gives constructive guidance
- You feel embarrassed if someone points out something you've said or done
- You take your own mistakes, whether large or small, extremely to heart
- You like to be right, and struggle when someone points out that you're possibly not

- You find it hard to read other people and you're not sure where to start with body language
- You often miss signs that those around you are going through a tough time
- You're often not sure what to say to someone who is upset or angry
- You often blame other people for problems, rather than understanding your own role
- Your days are often thrown up in the air by a rising emotion
- You often overthink things and always jump to the worst-case scenario
- You find it very hard to cope with change
- You have emotional tantrums or outbursts which you later feel embarrassed or ashamed of
- You find it hard to let other people in and as a result, you find relationships very difficult.

This isn't an exhaustive list, because the scope of EQ is so large. However, if you can nod along to several of them on a regular basis, then you have some work to do. Don't worry, however, that's what the rest of this book is about! Having low EQ isn't a sign of a failure or something wrong with you, it's simply a sign that you need to focus on improving your life. By doing so, you'll gain major benefits and you'll be far happier for it.

If you do prefer to take a test, there are several you can look into. The most common is the MSCEIT, or the Mayer-Salovey-Caruso Emotional Intelligence Test. This takes just over half an hour to complete and covers 141 questions. The areas covered include perceiving emotions, understanding emotions, facilitating thoughts, and managing emotions.

Whether you want an actual score to work with or an idea that there is work to be done, the outcome will be the same. Working on your EQ is never a waste of time. It means that you will gain your overall aim – improving your communication skills, shedding shyness, and being able to socialize more easily. The content of this book will work towards raising your EQ naturally, but being aware of it and understanding that EQ is a vital component of a healthy and happy life, means that you're already on the right track.

IMPROVING YOUR EQ

So, what can you do to increase your EQ?

Often, being aware of a problem means you're more focused on fixing it. Simply being aware that you have a problem with low EQ means that you'll be more switched on when it comes to recognizing your emotions and understanding others. It turns your attention outwards, and that's a great first step.

The content of this book will help you with increasing your EQ, but if you want some specific ideas on what else you can do to raise your level, there is plenty to suggest.

Use Mindfulness to Manage Emotions

A key cornerstone of EQ is recognizing and managing emotions. Mindfulness is an ideal way to do all of that. This is a process of becoming more 'in the moment'. When you practice mindfulness, you allow change to happen without worrying about it, you don't think about what you can't change or control, and you don't worry about what is to come. It's a sense of calm and serenity that will change your life.

Mindfulness can be practiced in many different ways, but meditation is the ideal starting point. Keeping your mind in the here and now can be very difficult at first, but stick with it. By doing so, you'll be able to be more aware of your emotions, you'll be able to recognize them, understand whether they're helpful to you or not, and you'll learn to give yourself a moment to control rising emotions, before acting out of anger, upset, or jealousy, etc. This is also a great way to stop your whole day from being derailed by a short burst of intense emotion.

Try to Focus on Empathy

Communication and relationship building requires empathy. Be mindful (there's that word again) of other people and what they might be going through. Look at body language, try and read whether someone is hiding something, check whether they're making eye contact, listen to their words and try and analyze how they're speaking, rather than just allowing words to float in one ear and out of the other one.

Try and put yourself in the shoes of others and understand that everyone is fighting their own battles. By doing so, you'll increase your level of empathy and you'll find it far easier to connect with those around you as a result. This yields real, lasting relationships.

Understand Your Emotional Triggers

Everyone has a set of personal emotional triggers, but the key is to know what they are and then minimize their impact on you, avoid them altogether, or face them and overcome them. So, what are your emotional triggers? What things, people, or situations get you riled up and cause you to feel a certain way? This doesn't have to be anger, although that's the most common emotion to cause bad actions. It can be upset, sadness, jealousy, regret, basically any negative emotion.

It's a good idea to keep a journal to help you identify your triggers. Look back over the day and note down any strong emotions you felt, including what was happening around the time, what you were thinking about, or what/who you encountered. You will probably start to see patterns emerging over time and once you have that information, you can work out how best to stop that trigger from having such a stronghold over you.

Develop a Positive Attitude

Positivity will literally change your life. People with a low EQ often have a default negative attitude, but that can be changed. Try reframing. This is a cognitive behavioral therapy technique that is used for a variety of different situations.

Whenever you recognize a negative thought entering your mind, stop, acknowledge it, and then replace that thought with something positive. Repeat it and stick at it, until your brain recognizes the positive before the negative.

For instance, if you think "I hate the rain", acknowledge that as a negative thought and replace it with "the garden needs the rain". If you think "Susan always seems to be angry with me", replace that with "I need to understand Susan a little better".

It won't happen overnight, but soon you will notice the first seedlings of a more positive mindset!

Manage Your Time More Effectively

Time management and stress management work hand in hand. A person with high EQ handles stress effectively but they also don't go out of their way to put themselves in stressful situations in the first place. You can't avoid all stress, because it's a part of life, but you can do what you can to manage your time and feel more in control.

Try writing a list of goals you want to achieve that particular day and work toward ticking them off your list. Try specific techniques, such as the Pomodoro Method, which allows you to work in short, sharp bursts, along with short breaks to refresh your mind. Have a list of prioritized tasks you need to complete every day and work towards achieving them. The more in control and organized you feel, the less stress you'll encounter.

CHAPTER THOUGHTS

This first chapter has been an introduction to the rather complicated yet fascinating world of EQ. You are trying to improve your communication skills and become a master socializer, but you can't do any of that if you don't understand the role EQ plays in your life.

Working on improving your EQ means that you're focusing upon reading other people in a more effective way. Your communication skills will improve as you develop a more empathic view towards others, and you'll feel more confident with each small success.

Changing something about you on a deep level often means delving into areas of life that you don't think have that much of a connection to one another. However, EQ and your overall future aims are so closely linked that understanding the subject is vital.

Think carefully about your own level of EQ and if you want to take a formal test, go for it. The bottom line is that test or no test, you need to work on your EQ if you want to become a better communicator. It's not just about the things you say, it's about how you read others and how you react to them – conversations are two ways things and by connecting with others more deeply, you'll find it far easier to learn more about them and communicate with them more naturally as a result.

SOCIAL SKILLS ARE IMPORTANT FOR LIFE SUCCESS

Throughout every situation you encounter in life, you'll need to use your social skills.

You'll need to communicate with people, you'll need to assess situations, read body languages and you'll also need to tap into the other aspects of EQ, which we talked about in our last chapter. Everyone has social skills, you're not born with a zero capacity to communicate in some way with other people, but the quality varies from case to case.

For example, you might meet someone who's fantastic at communicating. They don't care if they've never met the person, they have no issues with shyness, they're pretty confident in themselves, and they're loud and proud. That is someone with highly tuned social skills, perhaps a little too far towards the end of the scale if they're super-loud or a little too confident.

You'll also meet people who use their social skills well but feel they also need to improve. Nobody is perfect and we can all do better.

You might place yourself in that category, or you might feel that your social skills need some serious work. It doesn't matter what your starting point is, it's about putting forth the effort to make things better. Part of that is about understanding why social skills are such a staple part of life.

Yes, it's about communicating with other people but it's not just about hearing the words and taking them at face value. It's also not about just speaking. People say things they don't mean when they're trying to hide their true emotions, you included. Well-tuned social skills allow you to delve a little deeper and find out what's really going on. It's also about voicing your needs and concerns and being able to read other people effectively.

Of course, social skills are also about non-verbal cues, such as facial expressions and body language. Having good social skills means that you get your point over in the right way, without misunderstandings or concerns.

If you think back to the last chapter on emotional intelligence, you'll see how this all links into one giant circle. Being a good communicator means that your EQ is higher automatically, having high EQ gives you the confidence to be able to speak your mind, look for the real meaning in someone's words, by being able to read them properly, and it allows you to control your emotions and avoid those emotional outbursts that would otherwise threaten your day and potentially put you at loggerheads with someone close to you.

In this chapter, I'm going to press home the importance of social skills a little more. You can't be successful or totally happy in life without having good quality social skills. Without them, you'll miss out in such a big way. The hope is that by showing you how important these skills are, you'll gain even more motivation to push through and improve your own situation.

WHY ARE SOCIAL SKILLS IMPORTANT? THE 3 STARTLING TRUTHS

The startling truth is actually this statement – without good quality social skills, you cannot succeed in life, either professionally or personally. There will always be more you could have done, things you wish you'd said, a problem that totally escaped you, or something which was a major blockage for you to go on and achieve what you dreamed of. You'll live your life in regret, with the "what if" looming large. Life with a question like that is no fun.

So, what are the three startling truths about social skills?

#1 Employers are always on the lookout for employees who have good social skills

No matter how qualified you are for the job, if you're going up against someone who has excellent social skills and can communicate more articulately and clearly, they're probably going to get the job over you. You could have smashed the interview, done a fantastic presentation, but their superior social skills will give them an edge that you can't overcome.

Every single day in the workplace you're going to come up against problems, complaints, collaboration opportunities, and possibly even conflicts. Good social skills allow you to traverse every single one of those situations.

For me, speaking up in a meeting has always been something that filled me with dread. I had a vision in my mind of speaking up, and my voice sounding quiet and squeaky, or even croaky. People would laugh and ask me to repeat myself, and upon doing so, they would simply demand "louder girl!" I can feel the humiliation, even though the situation never actually happened to me. That is a prime example of poor social skills and although I've certainly gone on to improve since then, I still stop for a second when in a meeting and allow that fear to show itself, before realizing that if I'm going to keep winning, I have to push it away.

It doesn't matter if you have more talent in your little finger than the other people in your office; if you find it hard to communicate, if you have low EQ and you struggle with collaboration and you can't express yourself in a way you would like, you're never going to hit the career high notes. All of that studying and training will have been for nothing because, at the end of the day, the basics matter the most. Employers will always look for someone who has great communication skills – it's often on the job description.

#2 Good social skills expand your network

It stands to reason that if you're able to socialize and communicate well, you're going to have more friends, more connections, and great opportunities for networking. Business opportunities can appear at any time; you could be at a party and a close friend introduces you to someone they know. Before you know it, you're discussing a joint venture that could bring you great wealth and future growth opportunities. It really is that simple much of the time.

However, if you lack confidence and your social skills need work, these types of opportunities will often evade you.

Networking is often thought of as something you do with business cards in hand, but every day you speak to someone new, you're basically networking. If you tell them about what you do for a living, you're networking without even realizing it. Having the social skills to get out there and make opportunities means that your overall personal success, whatever that is to you, will be achieved. If you lack social skills, you're always going to be wishing for more.

From a personal point of view, having good social skills means you'll have a larger circle, or you'll develop closer relationships with those around you. The people you laugh with and socialize with might not be your very best friends, but you're able to talk, chat, laugh, joke, and basically spend time of value. This requires social skills.

Can you see how almost everything you do in life needs social skills to some degree? Even sending an email requires social skills; you might not be talking to them, but you're expressing yourself in words, which need to be carefully crafted to ensure that you get the right message over, without offending, sounding off-hand, or perhaps unknowledgeable. Everything requires social skills to some degree and when you lack them, or you have a lower level of them, everything is going to miss the mark, leaving you feeling unfulfilled and downright frustrated.

#3 Social skills give you a better quality of life

Feeling free to speak up, confident enough to speak your mind, and not having to worry about saying the wrong thing, it feels fantastic. It's not just about having those connections I've just mentioned, it's about your life generally being better.

A good social circle means more fun. Close relationships mean you're supported and safe. Being able to be there for those around you makes you feel good. The confidence to speak your mind and put your views across helps to build your self-esteem and when that is high, almost anything is possible!

When you have high class social skills, when your EQ is high, you will have a much better quality of life overall. No more crippling anxiety, no more shyness, no more turning down dates and parties because you're worried about walking into the room alone, and no more struggling to find your voice. All of that is a thing of the past and what is left is a relaxed, easy, free, and happy canvas on which you can draw the life you really want – then go ahead and create it.

CONQUER SOCIALIZING WITH THESE 4 SKILLS

In our next chapter, I'm going to go into some real depth on the skills you can use to build up your EQ and therefore the quality of your social skills, however, in this section, I'm going to briefly introduce you to them. By understanding why social skills are important you can move forward to start building up your own levels, but you need to know the work that is ahead of you.

There are certain things you can do every day, skills you can use in your daily life, which will give you a great head start. Soon enough, these things will become second nature to you, and you'll perform them almost without any thought whatsoever. When you reach that point, you'll also be able to pat yourself on the back because that's real progress right there!

So, what four skills can you use in your everyday life that will take you a long way towards conquering the art of socializing?

Empathy

In our last chapter, we talked about EQ and mentioned the ability to put yourself in the place of someone else. This is called empathy and by learning the art of empathy and pushing it forward into your everyday routine, you'll be able to understand other people far more effectively.

This is about knowing what someone needs to feel comfortable enough to open up, knowing that you should treat others as you would want to be treated, and it allows you to listen properly and really understand them at their very core. As you can see, socializing isn't just about talking, it's about understanding too.

Listening

You might think that listening is a super-easy thing to do. You just literally listen, however, it's a skill that most people fail to do effectively. Listening isn't just hearing the words and allowing them to float into one ear, spend a small amount of time in your brain, and then float back out the other side. It's about *really* listening. It's about tuning into what is said and what isn't said. It's about reading body language, assessing the way someone speaks, and it's about other people knowing that you're really listening because this will encourage them to open up.

Co-operation

It's very rare in the modern world that we work alone, and it's far more likely that you're going to be asked to work as part of a team at some point. This takes specific types of skills and it also means fully understanding what is expected of you and what your role is within that team.

Teams have a common goal to achieve and in order to achieve those goals, people need to work together well, be able to overcome misunderstandings and problems and focus upon that common goal above everything else. Again, don't worry too much at this point about the specifics of how to develop these skills right now, as we're going to explore that in far more detail shortly. For now, simply understand that these skills are very useful in your everyday life and will help you become a better communicator and socializer, whilst reaching your aims in life.

Positivity

How does positivity help you with socialization? EQ and positivity work hand in hand, but let's be honest, most people would rather be around positive people compared to negative people. This can be as simple as basic manners, remembering to say "please", "thank you", "good morning", etc.

The basics really do get you far and never underestimate the power of manners. Most people determine whether they like someone based firmly on how polite they are and how they use their manners, it's a sign of their decency, and when you remember this fact, whilst also pushing forward with a positive attitude, you'll be amazed at how much easier it is to work with people. Again, people respond far better to positivity!

We're going to delve into these skills in our next chapter but you can see that developing your social skills isn't really anything totally mind-blowing and it's more about knowing the basics and pushing forward, whilst building your confidence to the point where you feel much more comfortable going past your current comfort zone. Shyness doesn't have to be a barrier that holds you back throughout your life, it can be something that you overcome and allow to lead you forward to greater things in life.

EXPERT'S THOUGHTS ON SOCIAL SKILLS

Don't just take my word for it, the experts all agree that social skills are a key and integral part of life.

Humans are social beings. We crave togetherness and comfort, and in order to achieve that, we need to ask for what we need, and we need to give those things to other people. How do you do that? Via your social skills.

However, we live in a digital age and a lot of the time people, especially young adults, are communicating via social media and messaging apps, rather than actually speaking to people in person. That can be extremely detrimental and we're seeing rising levels of anxiety and depression amongst younger people, thought to be linked to this lower amount of socialization going on.

When we socialize with others on a regular basis, we increase our level of EQ, we show our empathy and develop this skill to a higher level, and we understand far more. We understand the views of other people and they understand ours; we can have constructive conversations about points which might be contentious, and develop a deeper understanding whilst also opening our minds to new approaches and different ideas. Having a high level of EQ and high-quality social skills means that you are more open-minded and agreeable to other people's views and that can never be a bad thing.

Experts also agree that social skills can literally make a business deal or break one. In the business world, it often comes down to the small things as to whether a deal is going to go ahead or not. A small misunderstanding can totally ruin a fantastic deal, and when your social skills aren't up to par, it's very easy to say the wrong thing without meaning to, perhaps not understanding how the other person might perceive what you're saying.

At the end of the day, humans need those key social interactions in life, whether on a personal basis or a professional. When your social skills are high quality, it's far easier to go out and meet new people, explain your needs to those around you, and deepen friendships and relationships with people already in your life. This simply makes life better and happier. It really is as simple as that.

Without those close connections, your life will always be on the fringes and your personal relationships will always be lacking something. Developing close relationships with other people hinges on social skills and that is something that all experts agree on, after years of research and studies.

For these reasons alone, and many more besides, focusing upon overcoming your self-limiting thoughts, on understanding your weaknesses and overcoming them, whilst kicking shyness to the curb, is something you should certainly focus your time and attention upon.

CHAPTER THOUGHTS

Social skills are so important for life, not only in terms of your success but also in how you develop relationships with other people. When you connect with others, life is more fulfilling, and you have that all-important circle of support around you. You cannot meet other people and create those connections without using your social skills at the start.

In this chapter we've really driven home the importance of social skills and why you need them for your personal and professional life. Use this information as a springboard towards your own success in mastering communication and improving your skills. Now you know why they're important and the basics to build on, you should be feeling motivated to make all-important changes.

3

THE CHALLENGES ENCOUNTERED – WHAT BLOCKS YOU FROM SOCIALIZING?

Your personal reasons for struggling with socializing might be completely different from everyone else who picks up this book, but it's important that you identify what they are. Without really knowing what you need to do, you're working in the dark!

For me, it was a fear of saying the wrong thing, of embarrassing myself, and of failing. Of course, that all came down to shyness, but maybe shyness isn't your issue.

In this chapter I'm going to talk about your own blockades, the walls you subconsciously put up to stop you from reaching out to others and socializing. You might think that's a harsh statement because you're not doing any of this on purpose, but without even realizing it, you're allowing your fears and your limiting beliefs to get in the way. The key is to know what they are and learn to overcome them. Handily, the advice in this book is going to give you plenty of tips on how to do that!

WHAT ARE YOUR PERSONAL MENTAL BARRICADES?

Shyness and social anxiety are two possible barricades that are stopping you from socializing, but these aren't the only two options. It could be that you have a very different mental blockage that simply needs to be knocked down in order to make a major improvement in your life.

Let's look at a few common barriers that may be in your way to socializing:

- **Jumping to conclusions** – If someone has a tendency to jump to conclusions without fully listening to what the other person is saying, this is a huge barrier to communication. Forming early judgments means that you're not present in the moment and the other person is going to feel not listened to and not taken seriously.

- **Poor focus and low attention span** – The inability to pay attention for too long can also be a barrier to communication and can be something that affects a person's ability to use their social skills to the best of their ability. This can be due to a number of reasons, but someone who suffers from ADHD may struggle to pay attention for too long; therefore, if a person is taking too long to get to the point, they won't be able to listen for quite as long as they would like.

- **Language barriers** – A language barrier is a huge problem in itself because this opens up the possibility of misunderstandings and a huge wall coming down between either party. It can also be the case that when a message is communicated, it loses its credibility and meaning and therefore, erodes away at its quality.

- **A lack of trust** – Communication has no space for distrust and if one of the people communicating doesn't trust the other one, there is going to be a huge barrier in the way. This basically means that one party pays very little attention to what the other person is saying and could also mean that they don't believe what they're saying. As a result, there is zero credibility to the conversation.

- **Emotions on the day** – How a person is feeling on any given day can greatly affect how they respond to others and how they communicate in general. If someone is feeling angry about something which happened earlier in the day, they can easily be short with the person they're speaking to, although completely unrelated in a topic. That can cause a higher chance of misunderstandings or the other person feeling that maybe they're angry at them. That's just one example, but how someone is feeling, and their general emotional state can cause a huge communication blockage. Great communicators try not to let their emotions get in the way of how they speak to people, but this is sometimes easier said than done! Of course, this is also where EQ comes into the equation.

As you can see, it's not always shyness or social anxiety that causes a person to struggle with communication and their social skills in general. A person who is struggling with their mental health, in general, will no doubt find that their ability to socialize is reduced, simply because their focus is affected. If someone is struggling with anxiety, that could cause them to become fearful or even paranoid about the intentions of those they're speaking to, which leads to the distrust mentioned earlier.

It's important to pinpoint what your particular barricade is. If it's social anxiety or shyness, that's something we're going to explore in more detail shortly, but give it some thought because these aren't always the only two options available to you. When you know what the problem is, you have more information to use in terms of knocking that barricade down.

SHYNESS VS SOCIAL ANXIETY – WHAT MAKES THEM DIFFERENT?

Many people lump social anxiety and shyness into the same category, but they're actually two distinctly different situations and deserve to be separated.

Many people with social anxiety go through life thinking they're shy, but it's actually a step up on the ladder and is actually considered to be a psychiatric disorder. The good news is that if you do suffer from social anxiety, it can be treated with cognitive behavioral therapy, however, recognizing the condition is the first step.

Shyness is feeling worried and fearful in social situations. Social anxiety is panicking and being fearful to another level. The conditions are so similar that it's hard to explain them with any real separation, but it really comes down to the severity of the effects that pull them apart.

The best way to explain shyness is a personality trait. Most people who are shy don't like having the spotlight on them and if they have to attend a social event when there is going to be any amount of attention on them, they become fearful and worried. However, shyness isn't usually debilitating, although it can hold you back in life if you allow it to do so.

On the other hand, social anxiety is a far more serious deal. A person with social anxiety will have distress on a completely different level to shyness when faced with a situation that causes them to be in the spotlight, and even when they're not in the spotlight. This could mean that they completely avoid social situations altogether, in order to try and feel better. You can understand why this would be damaging because we've already established that humans need to have social interactions in order to thrive, but also to have any amount of personal or professional success in life. In addition, social anxiety can cause a person to think that they're being judged at all times, or even watched. This can erode away not only their confidence but also their mental health.

The main symptoms of social anxiety include:

- Fast heart rate
- Feeling nauseous
- Shaking
- Sweating excessively
- Facial blushing
- Difficulty getting words out
- Extreme self-consciousness
- A fear of being judged
- Avoiding any type of social situation.

Shyness shouldn't be downplayed, however. Yes, it's less severe than social anxiety, but it can still play a major role in causing a person to avoid any type of socialization and to severely damage their quality of life.

3 TRICKS TO OVERCOME ANXIETY & SHYNESS

Overcoming anxiety and shyness certainly takes time and effort. No matter what you try, it's not going to work overnight. That's something you need to be prepared for. It's easy to start something and assume that you're going to see change overnight, but you'll be disappointed here. The key to overcoming anxiety and shyness is pushing yourself out of your comfort zone, facing fears rather than running away from them, and all of this takes time to build up. However, it's time well spent, that's for sure.

In this section, we're going to talk about three specific tricks you can try on a regular basis, building up your new-found immunity to anxiety and shyness.

Don't Run Away from Fear, Face It

When you're scared of something, the first instinct you have is to run away from it. This is a normal reaction because you just don't want to have to deal with it. Why should you want to? It's painful and it makes you feel bad. However, if you run away from your fears on a constant basis, you're going to find that they start to own you. How can you overcome something if you simply run away from it every time it rears its ugly head?

The problem with shyness and social anxiety is that the fear you have isn't actually rational. To you it's very real, it was to me, but in reality, when you look back on it, you wonder why you were scared. I often feel that way now. Back in the day, I was terrified of speaking in meetings. I'd do everything I could to avoid it, even trying to busy myself taking notes and trying to look busy, but did hiding away help me overcome that fear? Not at all. If anything, it just caused it to grow. I look back now and I can't believe I was so scared. Sure, I still don't love speaking up at meetings, it's not my most favorite thing in the world, but I'm not scared anymore. If I say the wrong thing I don't shrink back in embarrassment, I just laugh at myself.

If I can do it, so can you.

Facing your fears isn't easy, but the more you expose yourself to them, the less power they have over you and the less fearful you'll be.

Step 1 - Acknowledgment

The first thing you need to do is acknowledge it. What are you fearful of? What is it exactly? Give it a name. Be as specific as you can when you acknowledge it to yourself and if it helps, write it down.

"I am fearful of standing up in front of a group of people and speaking"

Then say why you're fearful.

"I'm scared my voice will crack and they'll laugh at me".

Whatever it is, name it.

Step 2 – Challenge Your Ideas

Why do you think that someone will laugh at you if your voice cracks? Why do you think that you should be scared when you stand up and speak in front of people? Do you think everyone else in the room is super-confident and nobody else has the same worry?

Challenging your ideas means pulling apart your fear and questioning it. Fear doesn't like to be questioned because when it is, it doesn't have the answers. Then, it loses its power because you realize it's nothing more than a very clever ruse.

If you're fearful of being rejected by a group of people, ask yourself why you're automatically going to be rejected. What is so terrible about you that every person you meet is going to be instantly repulsed? There is no answer to that because it's not the truth.

Really analyze and pull apart your fear and you'll quickly start to see that the very thing you were fearful of is nothing more than fear itself. The problem is nothing more than an idea and ideas aren't always right.

Step 3 – Face Your Fear

This is the hardest part, but the first two steps will have prepared you well.

You're reading this book because you don't want to be held back any longer. You want to be able to socialize freely and be happy in your relationships. So, you need to do the work and that means ripping off the Band-Aid and going for it. You can do it, don't tell yourself that you can't!

If you're scared of speaking up at a meeting, just do it. You don't have to give a speech, you can just put forth one short idea, but the more you do it, the easier it will become and the more you'll see that your fear was just imaginary. If you're fearful of being rejected by a group of people, embrace the wonderful person you are and just go in there and be yourself. You'll soon see that people are more welcoming than you're giving them credit for.

You can't just do this once. You have to keep facing your fear to pull away from its power and eventually you'll get to the point where you can't believe you were ever so scared.

Let's Play a Game

When facing fears and pushing yourself into situations that would otherwise cause you to feel anxious and allow your shyness to spike, it's a good idea to take yourself out of the situation whilst still doing it.

Confused? Let me explain a little more.

This game is going to help you do the things that you're worried about or fearful of, but you're not going to feel like it's you that's doing them. You're going to act. You're going to pretend you're someone else and dare yourself to do more. It's easier because it's not you who's doing it, it's your alias.

For this to work, you need to design your alias very carefully in order to really be in the moment. What do they look like? What are their character traits? What do they like and dislike? You're playing a character here so you need to be as detailed as possible when creating them, so you can play them to perfection. Pretend you're an actor getting ready for your latest role.

Once you know your alias well, transform yourself into them. Go on, try it! When you're not actually being yourself, it's easier. You might even find it easier to style yourself slightly differently, perhaps dress differently or do your make-up differently. Don't make it too 'out there', but do whatever you need to do in order to get into character.

Then, go for it. Do whatever it is that you're fearful of, but do it as the character you're playing, not yourself. Dare yourself to push it a little further and get your competitive spirit flowing. If you're scared to approach people you don't know and speak, dare yourself to do it twice and give yourself a pat on the back when you manage it. You could even bribe yourself with the promise of a reward later!

Practice Makes Perfect

Preparation is key when trying to overcome something. If you're getting ready to give a big presentation at work, you'd practice several times over to get it right. You need to adopt the same mindset to overcoming your socialization barriers.

Of course, practice means putting yourself out there and doing the one thing that scares you, but there are ways you can minimize the exposure and make it feel slightly less daunting to you. Here are a few suggestions.

- **Work on practicing non-verbal cues –**
  Communication isn't just about the words you say, it's also about gestures, body language, and the way you speak. You can practice those things whilst minimizing how terrifying it feels to you. If public speaking is your fear, start slowly by making sure that you're opening up your body language, keeping an eye on your facial expressions, and maintaining eye contact. Start watching the body language of other people too. This still means you're building up your social skills but you're doing so in a protected way.

- **Try to use activities along with conversation –**
  When you try to build up your social skills, you're going to be worried about holding a long conversation and you're going to be fearful of awkward silences. However, if you work towards situations that allow you to do something, e.g. you're part of an activity, you have something to busy yourself with whilst you're talking. For instance, you could

be at a sporting event. You're watching the game but you're also chatting.

- **Dare yourself on a daily basis** – Setting yourself a dare is a good way to keep on practicing. You could call this a goal if you prefer to avoid dares. All you need to do is set yourself a target of speaking to one person randomly per day. This means striking up a conversation. See how many days you can keep it up for and try and push your boundaries a little more every day.

Remember, overcoming shyness and social anxiety takes time and effort. I'm not going to lie to you and say it will be easy, but it will be the most worthwhile thing you'll ever do. Take small steps every day and before you realize it, you'll have walked more than a mile.

CHAPTER THOUGHTS

Whatever barrier is standing in the way of you improving your social skills, it's important to identify it, or the plural barriers if that's the case. Don't be down on yourself for whatever it is that you do acknowledge but use it as motivation to make changes.

In this chapter, we've talked at length about shyness and social anxiety, as well as what makes them different. Despite the fact that they certainly aren't the same thing, overcoming them uses a very similar approach. Your anxiety or your shyness does not own you. I know this myself. It feels like it does, but trust me, you're the one in control and all it takes is learning that fact to give you the courage and the strength to knock down those barriers.

4

ANALYZE YOUR CURRENT TOXIC SOCIAL HABITS & BEHAVIORS, THEN REVOLUTIONIZE THEM!

As we go through life, we pick up habits and behaviors that may not be useful to us. Of course, you pick up very positives ones too, but throughout the years you're walking on this Earth, you're going to absorb a few negative traits too.

The problem is until you address these traits and behaviors, you might have no clue that you have them. These traits and behaviors could be connected to the way in which you socialize, or don't socialize, and as a result, they could be contributing greatly to your problems. The key is to practice self-awareness and be more mindful of what you're doing when you're not actually paying attention.

Of course, from the point of view of EQ, having toxic traits is very damaging. For example, if one of your toxic traits is that you're always on your phone when you're with people you're supposed to be socializing with, you're not present in the moment. This lowers your EQ because you're not responsive to those around you or showing them the attention they deserve.

In this chapter, I want to turn your attention to the possible traits that might be dwelling within you, without your knowledge. This isn't something you should feel shameful of, but it is something you should take seriously. Once these traits are identified, you should do all you can to try and reverse them. This will have a very positive effect on your EQ and your ability to socialize with others.

I'll hold my hands up and say that I used to use my phone far too much. I'd go and meet friends and my phone would be on the table next to me. It was rude, but I didn't realize it at the time. It's only by looking at myself carefully that I identified this trait and worked to stamp it out. Now, I keep my phone in my bag and only take it out if it's a very important call. Being present in the moment is extremely important – people aren't going to want to talk to you if you're basically ignoring the time and attention they're giving to you.

So, let's look at a few of those traits and work out whether you have any work to do too.

LABELING TOXIC BEHAVIORS

When we talk about someone having toxic behaviors, that doesn't mean the person themselves is toxic, it means that they're showing behavior that isn't helpful and isn't respectful of others. If they don't realize they're doing it, you can help them to overcome their traits. However, if they know they're doing it and they simply continue, that's a whole other ball game that cannot be fixed without their will to do so.

The best gauge to know whether you've been around a person with toxic traits is to think about how you feel after you've been with them. Did you feel disappointed? Did you feel like it was a waste of time? Did you feel listened to? What did they do in particular that made you feel like the whole interaction was pointless?

Some common toxic traits include:

- Acting in a judgmental manner
- Taking up a huge amount of someone's time unnecessarily
- Refusing to take responsibility for their actions.

You might think that these aren't actually connected to communication but they're very integral to EQ, which is basically the same thing! If someone is judgmental, they're not showing empathy. If someone is taking up your time, they're not too bothered about what else you need to do and they're being disrespectful. If someone refuses to take responsibility for their actions, they're pushing the blame onto others and again, showing zero empathy.

Using your social skills links in so closely to EQ and any trait which negates that, also affects how you communicate with those around you.

Now, I'm not suggesting that you have any of these traits, but it's possible you do. Be honest with yourself. Do you do anything on a regular basis that could show other people that you're not taking them seriously? That you're not showing them empathy? That you basically don't want to give them the time of day? Again, no judgment here – perhaps you're not aware of it. However, it's easier to be aware of this in other people first and foremost and then become used to how it looks and feels. It's much easier to analyze yourself once you have a little background information as the victim, rather than the perpetrator.

THE TOXIC HABITS & BEHAVIORS THAT NOBODY WANTS

Everyone has a different idea of what toxic is, however, there are some common traits which most people would consider to be toxic. This section is going to take a good look at them in turn.

- **Focusing too much on yourself** – If you make everything about yourself, it's not only annoying but it's extremely off-putting to people around you. You want to build up your social skills, but you also need to be a person with whom others want to socialize. By making everything about you, you're not showing empathy to others.
- **Not listening to others** – Pushing your views onto other people, not listening to what they have to say, and assuming that you know what they're going to tell you without taking the time to hear them speak, these are all negative traits that have no place in the life of a person with high EQ and good relationships with those around them.
- **Being judgmental or critical** – Again, this means you're

not showing empathy. You don't have the right to judge or criticize anyone, because you're not living their life and you're not walking in their shoes. By doing so, your empathy has gone out of the window.

- **Blaming everyone for your problems** – People who push the blame onto everyone else and never take responsibility for their problems or issues aren't fun to be around. This can also be quite manipulative and border on narcissism. Let's face it, we all make mistakes and nobody's perfect – own it!

- **Not being present in the moment** – I've mentioned this one already, but if you're always off on another planet when people are speaking, distracted, or on your phone all the time, you're not present in the moment and you're not showing them respect.

- **Feeling entitled and showing it** – In this life, nobody is entitled to anything. We have to work for what we have and feeling like you're entitled to everything falling into your lap doesn't make you a great person to be around. You're not owed anything.

- **Using arrogance to hide fear or worries** – It's normal to be worried, to be fearful, or to feel inadequate but if you use arrogance to try and hide that, you're showing very negative communication styles and you're not going to endear people towards you. Be real. Show that you're not perfect, show that you're fearful sometimes. People respond far better to authenticity.

- **Being too competitive** – Being a little competitive is fine, but pushing others out of the way to get what you want isn't. If you're going to be competitive with anyone, be competitive with yourself by pushing yourself to meet your own goals. Don't make everyone your rival otherwise you run the risk of alienating people.

- **Jealousy** – Do you regularly allow the green-eyed monster into your life? If so, it's not going to endear you to anyone. Feeling envious is normal but allowing that to turn into jealousy is nothing short of damaging.

- **Being stubborn** – Refusing to do something out of pride or out of a so-called cause isn't cute. If anything, it will cause other people to become frustrated with you and that becomes a huge barrier to communication.

- **Holding on to grudges** – Do you hold onto grudges long after the initial problem is over? Everyone makes mistakes and that sometimes means that we say or do things we don't mean. By holding onto those issues and punishing those around you, you're just going to push them away. In the end, the only person who suffers is you.

- **Regularly playing the victim** – I'm going to talk about the victim mentality in greater detail later in the book but if you're someone who is always playing the victim, those around you are going to quickly become tired of it. You're in control of your life and whilst negative things happen in life, allowing them to make you feel and act like the victim on a constant basis isn't going to help you develop strong relationships.

- **Always being about the drama** – Do you gossip

regularly? Do you love drama? It's not a good thing to admit to. Being around someone who is always in the middle of a drama or someone who is always gossiping and trying to be into everyone else's business doesn't allow you to build up trust. Relationships will always be less than they could be because of that huge barrier between you. If you want people to trust you, you have to just be yourself and stop judging and talking about others. Drama is nothing but stressful anyway!

You can probably come up with a few other negative traits and behaviors that are on your list of things you dislike. However, these are some of the most common and some of the most damaging when it comes to the relationships and connections we have with those around us.

I should point out that everyone has bad days and that means that sometimes you might show one or two of the above traits. There is no issue when something happens just once or twice, but when it becomes a habit, you need to address it to stop it from turning into a major barrier.

EVALUATING SELF: DO I POSSESS THESE HABITS & BEHAVIORS?

We've talked about some negative traits and behaviors and you're probably building up a picture in your mind of what all of this looks like, but now it's time to be real. I've encouraged you to think about whether you have any of these, but now you really need to dig deep.

Don't be scared and don't be hard on yourself. The fact you're reading this book willingly shows that you want to improve. We all make mistakes, we all have traits we wish we didn't, and we all catch habits that don't help us. What sets you apart is that you're willing to change them.

So, how can you tell if you're exhibiting these toxic traits or qualities without really knowing about it? Let's look at a few signs to help you out. If you can nod along to several, that's a good indicator that perhaps you need to do some work. It's important to be honest with yourself when reading these signs also; don't push something aside just because it's uncomfortable. This entire journey is going to revolutionize your life, but you have to be willing to do the work, some of which won't be pleasant to you.

Signs You've Developed Toxic Habits or Behaviors

- Your friendships and relationships don't last long
- People seem to be distracted or show negative body language after spending any time with you
- Friends don't always share their good news with you
- You always have some drama going on in your life
- You've been described as a perfectionist or competitive
- You've been accused of being jealous more than once
- You often gossip about other people
- You don't say 'sorry' too often
- You bond with others by talking about people you both know
- You often consider yourself to be the victim in situations

- You're often quite needy and find it difficult to spend time alone
- You lose your temper quite easily
- You have a negative and pessimistic attitude
- In honesty, you take from people more than you give to them
- You use social media as a way to fish for attention
- You rarely see how your problems are caused by you, and you blame everyone else
- You always like to be right
- You find it hard to accept someone else's opinion as just as valid as yours
- You take everything quite personally
- You often need validation in order to feel good or as though you've succeeded

You might have one or two traits to work on, or you might have a whole bunch. The number doesn't matter right now, but your attitude towards it does.

LET'S GO FROM TOXIC TO HEALTHY

You might be feeling pretty down after reading the above list, depending upon how many traits you can tick off. It's time to plaster on a smile because there is plenty you can do about it. Moving from toxic to healthy is entirely possible and the more you try, the easier it will become.

Many people who struggle with social skills and communication are bogged down with not only possible shyness or social anxiety, but also several barriers that they place in front of themselves. In order to make life a little easier, they develop negative traits as a coping mechanism but these work against them, rather than for them. By identifying these traits, you can work out what you need to stop doing and then focus on the right kinds of techniques instead.

So, how can you turn your toxic traits into something totally healthy? Here are a few ideas.

Fake a Smile

Go on, try it. It's not possible to smile and not feel slightly more uplifted than you did before. When you smile more often, you'll also see that those around you respond to you differently too. We're far more likely to talk to people who smile and look approachable than someone who is frowning and looks troubled. So, plaster on that smile, even if you don't feel like it, and wait for the good vibes to spread.

Keep a Gratitude Diary

This is a very useful technique for a variety of different problems, but it helps you to avoid negativity and that annoying victim mentality. By being grateful for what you have, you feel uplifted, happier, and comforted within yourself. All you need to do is write down one or two things you're grateful for out of any particular day, every evening. You'll soon see that there are more positive in your life than you're aware of.

Avoid Being Sucked into Gossip

You have a choice whether you gossip about someone else or not – nobody is making you backchat. You have the power to excuse yourself from any conversations that feels negative and that are characterized by talking about other people.

Learn to be aware of when you're gossiping, stop yourself, and mindfully change the subject. Remember, talking about other people says more about you than it does about them.

Do a Good or Kind Deed Every Day

The more good we do, the more we want to do. In addition, when you do a good deed for someone or you show kindness that makes them smile, it makes you feel good too, increasing your confidence and your empathy. Every single day, aim to do something good for another person, even if it's just complimenting them on their sweater. However, make sure that whatever you say or do is done with the best intentions and not simply to tick an item off a list.

Learn to Laugh at Yourself

Taking yourself too seriously isn't going to make your life very happy or fulfilling. We all make mistakes and do silly things occasionally, but that doesn't mean we should beat ourselves up about them. Learn to laugh at yourself and your mistakes, and you'll be less overcome with self-hatred and upset whenever something doesn't go your way.

Take a Break from Social Media

The very thought of logging off your social media accounts for a week might fill you with dread but trust me, it's a very useful tool. We are all far too obsessed with what everyone else is doing, thinking, and the validation we seek from our followers. It's time to focus on yourself, those around you, and learn to only look for validation from within. Taking a break from social media will allow you the chance to reconnect with yourself. Let's be honest, social media is nothing but drama anyway.

Stop Trying to Take Control of Everything

Perfectionism isn't a good thing, no matter what you might have taught yourself to believe. By trying to control everything, you're not allowing yourself to live in the moment or to experience the joy of spending time with those close to you. Stop, slow down, take your hands off the wheel, and just allow yourself the chance to drift for a while. If you find yourself going off course too much, you can easily correct your direction. Chill out and go with the flow a little!

Learn to Use Positive Affirmations

Never underestimate the power of positive affirmations. They might feel a little odd at first, but they are one of the best tools to help you develop a positive mindset. Choose an affirmation that really resonates with you and repeat it several times a day, when you wake up, when you go to bed, and at any point in the day when you feel your resolve shaking.

Your affirmation can be anything. "I am able to do whatever I set my mind to", "I am a strong and kind person", "I am willing to deal with whatever comes my way with positivity and success" are just a few suggestions but you can choose whatever you want. Head online for plenty of inspiration or just make up your own.

Stop Blaming Everyone Else for Your Problems

There may be some problems in your life that really aren't your fault, but they're not anyone else's either. Stop pushing the blame onto others because by doing so, you're creating a toxic energy that causes people to steer clear of you. Instead, accept your problem and create a plan to overcome them, using your new positive affirmation to stay on the right track.

Be Mindful of How You Speak to Others

For a while, be very mindful of the verbal and nonverbal language you use when speaking to other people. You might have picked up a habit of using closed body language, avoiding eye contact, or being sarcastic, without even realizing it. The only way to identify it is to be mindful and observe yourself. Once you recognize a negative communication trait, be even more mindful to stamp it out. If you catch yourself doing it again, stop, change course, and over time, it will become second nature to avoid it.

Keep Your Complaints to Yourself

A little earlier I suggested keeping a gratitude diary and that should help a lot with this particular suggestion too, but you need to stop complaining! It's very likely that people are avoiding spending time with you if you're constantly complaining about everything that's going wrong in your life. It literally sucks the energy out of people! Reframe those complaints and remember that there is always someone worse off than you.

None of these action points are hard to do and you can start working on all of them right now. Even if you don't have a huge number of toxic traits to stamp out of your life, using these techniques can really help you to increase your EQ level, which will of course help to boost your social skills too.

CHAPTER THOUGHTS

As we move through life, it's easy to pick up habits that are perhaps more negative than they are positive. Whilst it's never a good thing to just carry on using them willy-nilly, it's sometimes difficult to stop and take stock of what you're doing without being extremely mindful in the process.

Using toxic habits and behaviors will not help you to become a better communicator and it won't allow you to build relationships and the social circle you crave. However, you can quickly identify the problem, or problems, and work to eradicate the issue. Rather than becoming down or having these traits, pat yourself on the back for admitting it and get to work.

II

PRACTICAL STEPS YOU CAN TAKE TO CONQUER SOCIALIZING

5

MAKE THE BEST FIRST IMPRESSIONS POSSIBLE

Welcome to the second part of our book!

The first part was all about emotional intelligence, why social skills matter, and really raising awareness of the journey you need to take. This next part is going to be practical, action pointed, and it's going to give you lots to work on in order to really start seeing major improvements in your relationships with those around you, your confidence levels, and how you interact with other people.

In this chapter, I want to talk about a very important aspect of communication – the first impression.

THE FIRST IMPRESSION LASTS

Think of the last time you developed a first impression of something or someone. Did you find it easy to shake that first impression, even if you were proven incorrect in your assumption later down the line? Probably not.

First impressions stick. We make them quickly, we assume they're correct, and they're very hard to overcome once they're solidified in your mind. Even if that thing or person does something to make you think that perhaps you were wrong about them, you still have a niggling doubt in your mind afterward, simply because of the impression you made right at the start. It's for this reason that businesses place such a huge amount of importance on marketing strategies that really hit the right mark. If you allow your customers to think the wrong thing about you, they're just going to go to one of your competitors instead.

In terms of your personal communication style and social skills, first impressions matter just as much. This is vital in both your personal life and your professional life.

The psychology of first impressions is quite interesting to learn about.

It is thought that you have just a few seconds to make your impression on someone. In this time, you're being judged for your trustworthiness, your integrity, your attitude, and unfortunately, also your attractiveness. After that, a deeper conclusion is formed, more about personality traits than anything else at this stage. This happens over just 3 seconds.

All of this occurs because of something called cognitive bias and that forces someone to make a quick-based judgment upon you. That judgment may be entirely correct, or it might be very far from the mark. It's worth noting that these judgments can also be affected by a person's stereotypical thoughts, so sometimes it's not entirely your fault if someone gets the wrong first impression of you. However, if the judgment is negative and incorrect, changing it takes far longer than the time it took to make the judgment in the first place.

Cognitive bias is what happens when you're quickly processing and coming to a conclusion about what is happening around you, but that conclusion can be affected to a large degree by your confidence levels, whether you're a positive or negative person and situations you've encountered before. Basically, it can't be relied upon entirely, but we do so because we believe what we tell ourselves.

To throw another term into the mix, we also have the primacy effect. This is the reason why a negative first impression lasts. The brain remembers things in sequence order, so when you encounter a person or a thing for the first time, that's the first step in your sequence, however, you'll always remember the first step more than any of the others. It's easy when you think about it – we remember our first love, the first time we tried out our favorite food, the first time we went to a certain place, etc. That means if someone meets you for the first time and they gain a negative first impression, rightly or wrongly, that's the first thing they'll remember about you when they come into contact with you again.

Of course, by making a snap judgment such as this, it also affects whether that person wants to be around you again in the future and how they treat you. On the flip side, if you make snap judgments about others incorrectly because you gained a bad first impression of them, it will affect how you communicate and interact with them too.

Can you see how important first impressions are? They're a very easy way to be misunderstood or misunderstand someone else and they affect so much more than just that one moment.

Your journey towards mastering communication and social skills has to incorporate first impressions. If you avoid this or ignore it and assume it's not important, you're not going to get very far with your journey.

The impression someone has of you isn't always about what you say, but also about how you present yourself. As humans, we focus a lot on faces, and that's likely to be because when we're very young, we watch the facial expressions of our parents to work out whether we're about to be fed, etc.! That habit tends to stick with us throughout life, so it's definitely worthwhile remembering that it's not all about what you say but often how you show yourself to the world. It can also be about how you do things, e.g. your choices and your competencies.

Let's look at a few examples.

- A person who is scowling will probably be considered unfriendly and unapproachable, but someone who is smiling and has a soft facial expression will be considered warm and approachable
- A person who runs up the stairs will be considered active and healthy, but a person who takes the elevator might be considered lazy
- A person whose hair is a little unkempt may be considered lazy or even dirty, but a person whose hair is neat and tidy,

presenting themselves in clean clothes will be considered professional and clean

Can you see how your habits and how you show yourself to the world is part of the deal too? It might seem like a lot to remember, but much of it comes down to common sense. Simply focus on being well turned out every day, clean, tidy, and be mindful of how your facial expression may be judged by others.

LEAVING THE BEST FIRST IMPRESSION

In order to build up professional connections and personal relationships, you need to know how to make those positive first impressions. This will make your social life so much easier and you won't be constantly backtracking, trying to correct an incorrect opinion someone has gained of you. You'll also find that you are successful in opportunities without failing and having to learn what you did wrong the first time.

There are countless times when you'll need to make a first impression, in fact, you might even have a few in the space of a day. For instance, a job interview is one of the most common and most terrifying times you need to make a good first impression, but how about if you attend a party? Whilst you might not relish the idea of speaking to new people at a party, by the end of this book you'll be doing it more than ever before! However, you'll need to make a good first impression on those people for your efforts to work.

So, how can you make sure that you're leaving the best first impression when you're socializing? Let's look at five important steps.

Be Mindful of How You Speak

The words you say and how you say them are two of the most important aspects of making a good first impression. It sounds complicated but it actually comes down to the basics more than anything else.

For instance:

- Remembering someone's name shows that you're taking them seriously and you value their input, and you're not passing them off as someone unimportant.
- Manners are vital – most people will form a very poor impression of someone who doesn't use 'please' and 'thank you' and who doesn't treat people with respect so always be mindful of this. Remember, manners cost nothing!
- Using too much slang and not speaking correctly can also work against you. Whilst nobody expects you to speak the Queen's English, you should avoid talking as though you're a grumpy teenager. You've never met this person before, so you need to show that you're someone who is interesting enough to strike up a conversation with.
- Try not to say 'erm', 'um' and 'ah' too much. Whilst it's normal to use in the odd occasion, saying these too often will just show that you're nervous, you're not sure what to say, and could even tell the other person that you don't really know what you're talking about. Try and appear confident, even if you're not.

- Try not to speak too fast or too quietly. Again, this shows that you're not confident or at ease. Slow things down and give yourself the time to think as you're speaking. That will automatically give you more confidence and also avoid the other person not being able to really understand what you're saying.

- Avoid using words that are overly complicated and that the other person might not understand. For instance, if you're speaking to someone about your job or another area of expertise that you're familiar with and they're not, don't litter the conversation with technical jargon. You're alienating them by doing this because they can't be expected to understand this subject as well as you, and they'll feel annoyed about it too. That is going to show them that you're not on the same level as them and they'll form a poor impression because of their experiences.

Put Your Phone Down!

I've mentioned this one several times before and we're all guilty of it occasionally, but keep your phone in your pocket or in your bag. In this digital age, we're constantly connected and switched on and it's extremely easy to lose yourself in the virtual world, whilst completely missing the real world around you. By doing so, you're letting people know that you're not interested in what they have to say and that you're quite rude and ignorant of their presence.

If you're waiting for an important call, just keep your phone in your pocket and put it on vibrate. That way you'll know when the phone is ringing, and you can excuse yourself outside to answer it. Constantly checking your social media accounts, emails, or generally scrolling through the news is not going to endear you to anyone and it's just going to make you look plain rude. Nobody likes rudeness.

Be Punctual

A positive first impression can be as easy as showing up on time. If you make someone wait for you, they're going to assume that you don't respect their time and that you deem them unimportant enough to show up when you're supposed to. Again, it's rude and it's one of the biggest bug-bears for most people.

A little earlier I mentioned manners and being punctual really ties in with this. For many people, bad manners are a deal-breaker, and they are for me too. I know if someone turns up late and then just doesn't seem to be very polite, I'm not going to like them very much and it's going to take a lot to change my mind. It doesn't take a huge effort to be on time, and if you do find that you're running late and you can't do anything about it, have the respect to call the person and explain, so they're not hanging around waiting for you.

Dress Comfortably Yet Impressively

I'm a big believer that you should dress for yourself but there is a very big difference between wearing slouchy, unkempt clothes at home when there is no-one around, and wearing them outdoors when people are unfortunately going to judge you. Such clothes will inevitably lead people to the wrong first impression of you, assuming you don't really care much about how you look.

For that reason, dress for comfort but also dress for style. Make sure that what you wear is suitable for the place you're going to and make sure that you feel good within it. If you feel good, you'll be more confident and that will help you to speak and socialize with fewer barriers between you.

I don't have to tell you about clothes that aren't the best idea versus ones that are, I'm pretty sure you know how to dress yourself appropriately, however, do be mindful in professional situations. There are no rules that women have to wear skirts and men have to wear suits but do make sure that you always look very well put together and you're not overstepping any imaginary lines, e.g. wearing skirts that are too short, or wearing suits that are too tight. Just make sure that you look professional and you feel comfortable within it.

If you're attending a party or a social gathering and you want to try out your social skills, what you wear does matter. People do notice these things almost instantly, probably as you walk into the room. So again, wear something comfortable but also something which shows you in your best light and doesn't place unnecessary negative attention upon you.

It goes without saying that you should always be clean and tidy, but again, I don't have to tell you that.

Be Aware of Your Body Language

The final step to making the best first impression possible is your body language. I'm going to cover all the do's and don'ts of body language in a later chapter, so I'm not going to dwell on it too much here. However, be aware that your body language does cause a person to decide upon their judgment of you very quickly indeed.

People with high EQ can read body language almost instantly. For instance, a person who is avoiding eye contact, crossing their arms over their body and fidgeting looks nervous and as though they're either trying to avoid something or they're lying. That's not the best first impression.

All you need to do is make sure that your body language is open and relaxed. That means making eye contact regularly (although, don't try and stare them out), you keep your arms relaxed by your sides and not over your body, you smile, nod along to what they're saying, and you avoid being too stiff or tense. Just relax into the moment and avoid fidgeting.

THE FIRST ISN'T THE LAST

Despite the fact that first impressions are very important, don't worry too much if someone does form a negative first impression of you. There are still chances for you to change that perception of yourself, although it's always better to get it right the first time!

Of course, this depends upon you knowing what you did wrong; they're unlikely to simply tell you, so being aware of how you come across to other people is key. Using the tips in the last section will allow you to do that and you'll become more self-aware as a result. Once you know what you did wrong, work to change it by showing them what you can do right and showing them a different side. For instance, if you appeared unkempt and tired the first time they met you, make sure that you are better turned out the second time and that you're more energetic and friendly. Once won't be enough, however, so you'll need to keep showing that positive side of your character to the point where their first impression is challenged enough in their minds.

Most researchers agree that it takes around eight positive situations to change a negative one. So, if you gave someone the wrong first impression, you'll need to show them around eight times (it's not an exact number) that their first impression was a little off-key.

That simply means being polite, using your manners, being friendly, smiling, making eye contact, watching your body language, and making sure it's positive, and being well turned out. These things aren't difficult but for someone who is struggling with their social skills, trying to remember it all can be difficult. My advice is to just focus on treating people in the way you would like to be treated. If you do that, you can't go wrong.

However, there may be situations when you really got off to a bad start with someone and something needs to be explained in order to push the metaphorical elephant out of the room. If you really feel like you need to explain why you came over so negatively, e.g. you were very snappy and rude, ask the person if you can have a quick word and apologize for your negativity and explain that you were caught off guard due to a personal issue. You don't have to go into more detail than that, you don't have to explain, and you only need to apologize once. Let it go after that and carry on being a positive and happy person that they want to spend time with.

Whilst first impressions are undeniably important, it's not a case of sudden death if you get it wrong. You can redeem yourself, although it's always better to not have to.

CHAPTER THOUGHTS

Making a good first impression on someone helps to build up a positive interaction and could lead towards friendship. However, if you give off a bad vibe during a first impression, you're going to have to work harder to put it right. It's far better to be aware of how you come over to other people and avoid this from happening.

A lot of the work that goes into making a good first impression is about the basics. Be polite, be on time, make sure your body language isn't going against the words you're saying, and simply be aware of the fact that on some level, whether they're aware of it or not, you are being judged.

6

HOW TO DEVELOP RAPPORT WITH ABSOLUTELY ANYONE

O ur last chapter served as the first practical step towards actually going out there and having fulfilling conversations with other people. That first impression is very important but to have a good conversation and to be able to use your social skills to their highest level, you need to build up something else – a rapport.

A rapport is an understanding or connection that two people, or a group of people, have with each other. This enables them to read the other person, to understand what they're thinking and feeling, and to be able to converse in an easy and friendly way. When you have a rapport with someone, communication is easy and smooth, and whilst there might be the odd awkward silence (inevitable, even for the most high-quality communicators) they won't faze you or cause the discussion to be disjointed or thrown off track.

Building up a rapport with someone doesn't always mean that you need to have a lot in common, but it is important. Let's explore why in this next chapter.

CONNECT WITH OTHERS: THE IMPORTANCE OF RAPPORT

We know that rapport is a connection of some kind, but how deep does that connection need to be? Not very. Colleagues can have a rapport simply because they work in the same place, they have something to talk about and they have a common goal to work towards. Friends have a rapport because they have a pre-existing connection, but strangers can also develop a rapport. It can be something as simple as commenting on the weather, "raining again, I hate rain!" and the other person says "yes, I really don't like it too" – the starting blocks of a rapport!

Rapport can happen without really much effort. If you've ever met someone and just instantly clicked, or "hit it off", that's an instant rapport. However, it's not like that for everyone and sometimes you have to work a little harder. It's likely to be the case that some people you just click with and others you don't, but that doesn't mean you can't build up a rapport with those people and look forward to fulfilling conversations and interactions.

Rapport is important not only in your personal life, with friends, family members, and strangers you strike up a conversation with on the street, but also in your working life too. An employer is far more likely to employ a person who they believe will fit in well with their current staff. Again, that harks back to the importance of social skills because being able to fit in and build up a rapport basically means you have strong social skills.

Rapport will also help you when working as part of a team when you're brainstorming and collaborating or simply when you're in the office or workplace in general. Rapport means that you have an understanding with someone or with a group of people and that can begin as small talk.

You might be someone who hates small talk, in fact, the chances of that are high. I used to hate small talk to the point where I used to avoid going to the hairdressers for as long as possible. However, small talk doesn't have to be excruciating and over time, it can actually be fun. Small talk allows you to search for the common ground you have with someone, such as hating the rain or being a big fan of chocolate. It can be absolutely anything, but the more you have in common with someone, the greater your rapport will be.

However, not having a huge amount in common with someone doesn't mean you can't build up that rapport, it just means you'll need to try harder.

Now we know what rapport is and why it is important, let's look at a few ways you can look to build up a rapport with people you meet.

EVERYONE IS ADMIRABLE, AND YOU SHOULD TELL THEM HOW

Everyone loves a compliment, whether they want to admit it or not! The single best way to build up a rapport with someone is to pick out something you admire about them and tell them. You don't have to gush about their amazing personality or how much you admire their work ethic; you can just tell them that you like their hair color or say you like their t-shirt and ask where they got it from.

The point here is that you're moving towards starting a conversation but you're doing so on a positive footing. You're not walking in there and complaining about something and then building a rapport based on something completely negative (never a good thing), and instead, you're moving towards building up that rapport from a positive point of view. The conversation obviously won't be all about whatever it is you admire about them, but it's a starting point and from there you will both feed off of one another to keep things going.

Before you panic, yes I know, small talk and keeping a conversation going is terrifying when you're not the greatest communicator in the world but practice really does make perfect. Not all conversations are going to be stilted and difficult. Some will flow and move from the topic with ease. The more you build your social skills, the more of the latter type of conversation you'll have in your life.

The key to giving compliments to start a rapport is to not make it sound like you're being over the top, that you're sugarcoating it, or that you're trying to suck up to them. You don't want to sound false and you want to make your compliment sound genuine. For that reason, only choose something which you genuinely admire. If you really detest their coat, you're not going to compliment them on it because your facial expression or your tone of voice is probably going to give you away.

If you really can't think of anything you want to compliment them on without it sounding false, you can rely on one other subject – the weather. "It's a lovely day, isn't it?" As with the comment about the rain earlier, it's a great way to connect but it's always better to focus on a positive comment, rather than a negative one, i.e. avoid "I don't like", "it's horrible", it's bad". These types of phrases will get the job done but they could hamper the first impression that the other person has of you – you're going in with a negative comment, so does that mean you're quite negative yourself?

YOU, ME, AND OUR HUMANITY

Common ground is vital if you want to not only start a conversation but also keep it going. When we have something in common, it's almost like a small light is ignited inside us and we become excited. We want to talk, we want to connect – we're humans, we're social beings whether we realize it or not!

A little earlier I mentioned that some people you meet will be supremely easy to speak to and others a little more difficult. This is because some people you have more in common with than others. It might be that you don't have a lot in common personality-wise but maybe you have a shared experience you can base the conversation on or a set of circumstances that you both share.

Again, we're going back to small talk. This helps you find that common ground by doing a little gentle digging but you're best sticking to non-contentious subjects. Don't go straight in there and ask their opinion about politics, religion, money-related subjects, or a very controversial subject on the news. Keep it light and non-inflammatory. You don't know this person yet and they might have very strong views which can be ignited very easily!

The most important thing to remember is that you're a human speaking to another human. They're not a monster, they're not a superhero, they're a human being just like you. It might scare you to start having conversations with people you don't know, but how do you know they're not thinking the same thing as you? Someone has to make the first move if a conversation is going to start and that might as well be you. It's entirely possible that the other person is waiting for you to go ahead and say something, so they know that you actually want to talk to them.

Rely upon your humanity and look towards theirs. If all else fails, inject a little humor to lighten the moment.

TALK ABOUT THEM (NO, NOT BEHIND THEIR BACKS!)

Finding common ground is easier if you ask questions of the person, but that doesn't mean firing question after question at them and making them feel like they're in an interrogation.

By shifting the focus of the conversation away from you, you'll probably feel a lot calmer and find it easier to talk, and by turning the focus
on the person, they'll feel like you're genuinely interested in them and
learning more about them.

Of course, in the moment it can be hard to come up with questions
and your mind is likely to go blank. For that reason, having a few easy
go-to questions in your armory will help you and will give you
confidence.

Here are a few generic questions you can save to the back of your
mind when you're in need of a quick conversation starter.

- The weather is great today, don't you think?
- I love animals, do you have any pets?
- Do you have any plans for the weekend?
- Have you been busy at work today?
- What kind of music do you like to listen to?
- Do you enjoy your job?

As you can see, finding common ground means asking very simple
and generic questions that allow you to learn more about the person.
From there, you can work out whether you have any common ground
you can use to move the conversation forward and build up that
important rapport.

There is one thing to be aware of here. When asking questions make
sure that you separate questions by using filler. This means giving
your own answer to the question and using that dreaded small talk.

For instance, let's look at asking "do you have any plans for the weekend?"

Your conversation partner will answer and say yes or no and probably elaborate on what those plans are to some degree. Rather than going straight to another related question, make sure that you give a little information about your own plans. Don't go into huge detail, but simply say "that sounds great, I think I'm going to have a relaxing one with my partner", as one example. By doing that, you're not firing question after question at them and probably scaring them somewhat!

ADJUST THE CONVERSATION

A little earlier I mentioned that some conversation topics can be a little difficult for some people and topics such as religion, culture, and politics, in particular, can be quite sensitive for many people. It's best to avoid these if at all possible but you might hit upon a difficult topic without realizing it. For instance, you might accidentally speak about an experience you've had which the other person finds distressing because of their own personal experiences. You have no way of knowing about that because you don't know the person.

In that situation, you need to stay calm and simply adjust the conversation slightly, diverting attention away from the sensitive subject and moving it towards something more mainstream. The weather is a great option here, but you have to do it in a way that is seamless and doesn't make it look like you're working towards damage limitation.

You'll understand that you've hit upon a difficult topic by reading the other person. This is where empathy comes to the fore. Watch the person's body language – if they tense up, if they don't make eye contact, or simply seem uncomfortable, the likelihood is that they're not entirely comfortable with the topic you've ventured towards.

Be receptive to the differences in their body language and their general stance and be ready to adjust the conversation accordingly. You don't have to do a quick U-turn, but you can simply redirect your chat towards something less contentious. A good reroute here is a compliment, just as you started the conversation. This may shake them out of their "moment" and put the chat back on course. Either way, simply changing the conversation is enough because by doing that, you're showing the other person that you've recognized their discomfort and you want to help them move past it. They'll be grateful and they'll no doubt do their part to keep the conversation flowing on, past that particular subject.

OPEN MINDEDNESS IS THE KEY

The most important thing to remember when conversing with anyone is that you should not judge, you should not allow your perceived ideas to cloud your mind, and you should certainly place stereotypes to one side. Put simply, you should be open-minded.

Being open-minded is the key to quality conversations that help to build connections. By being more open to talking to people you probably wouldn't otherwise speak to, you might learn something new, you might find a new friend that you can build up a fantastic rapport with, and you will be able to increase your social skills and build your EQ.

As humans, we tend to judge people very harshly and very quickly, especially in today's society. This does nothing for our connections with other people because we're too busy assuming that someone isn't going to be our type of person, so therefore we shouldn't try to speak to them. We might also become fearful of them because they look a certain way or belong to a certain culture or religion. These are all thoughts and ideas which need to be cleared from your head.

Every single person is worth getting to know. You don't know who you might connect with until you've attempted to look for common ground and build up a rapport. Avoid close-mindedness by simply seeing a person as a human being and blank canvas of stories, experiences, and fun that you might really enjoy getting to know.

Once you start to see people in that way, life becomes more fun because who knows who you could meet. You could meet the love of your life, your new best friend, or simply someone with who you have a really great conversation. You might learn something, you might not, but either way, being open-minded allows you to become a better person and allows you to connect with those around you more easily.

CHAPTER THOUGHTS

Building up rapport not only gives you the confidence to take conversations further, but it's the first step towards building relationships with people, either professionally or personally. We all have some amount of common ground, it's simply that in some cases you have to dig a little deeper to find it.

Practice using small talk, complimenting people, and using questions to try and find out what you may have in common and once you hit gold, use that subject to deepen the connection.

7

THE LIFE-CHANGING ABILITY TO DEVELOP FRIENDSHIPS WITH EASE

F riendships really do make life easier, more fun, and generally more rewarding. A life without friends is dull and you'll probably feel like you have to take on the world yourself, without any support.

However, meeting new friends can be a huge challenge for someone who lacks social skills and who finds communication difficult. The good news is that like all the topics in this book, this can be overcome, and you can look forward to meeting plenty of new friends, provided you open yourself up to the possibility.

Not everyone is going to end up being your friend, but that doesn't mean that you can't have great connections with them in the short-term, even if it is just one conversation. However, knowing how to move towards making connections with friendship potential is important and it's easier than you might think. That's what we're going to focus on in this chapter.

GETTING THE SOCIAL LIFE YOU'VE ALWAYS DREAMED OF

I used to regularly watch the TV show "Friends". I used to long to have that kind of close-knit group of friends who backed each other up through thick and thin, who never laughed at one another, who always supported each other, and who could always be depended upon to be there for either a good night out or a quick chat on the phone.

Whilst this type of social circle doesn't happen for many people, even those who are great socializers, it is possible to have a social life that is fulfilling, surrounded by people you really do call friends. It's important to remember that not everyone you meet will turn out to be who you think they are, and that sometimes you might find yourself led astray by someone with ill intentions, but these are all lessons you will learn as you start to navigate life with an active social element. For every bad one you meet, there are several good ones in their place and it's better to place the focus on experience and enjoyment, than trying to collect a set number of friends in your life.

It can be very hard to meet friends as someone who struggles with socializing. You put yourself into your own little bubble and close yourself off to some degree, I know I did. This doesn't make it easy to meet people and it makes it almost impossible for other people to see you for the warm and friendly person you really are.

The more you build up your social skills, the easier you'll find it to socialize for fun and as you do this, you'll find that you meet new people who end up being your friends. Whether they remain friends for life or for just a season remains to be seen but building up your social life will certainly become easier as you put in a little more effort.

FRIENDS, AND WHERE TO FIND THEM

If you want to meet new friends, you have to get out there and go to places where potential fits might be mingling themselves. Of course, it's better to try and meet people who have the same kinds of interests as you and in that case, think carefully about how your key interests can take you out of the house and into situations where other people are likely to be.

It's easy to think that you should sit at home and live your life online because it seems easier and safer, but by doing that you're not actually getting out and testing your social skills at all. Hiding behind a keyboard isn't fun and it's not going to help you build up emotional connections – the connections you have with people you meet online aren't going to give you the same fulfillment unless those connections translate to the outside world. Even then, safety has to be a concern.

For that reason, where can you go to meet people who have the same kinds of interest as you? If you enjoy crafts, can you go to a night class to learn more about a potential craft you might enjoy and meet other like-minded people? If you enjoy dancing and keeping fit, how about joining a Zumba class and meeting other dancer types? If you enjoy trivia, why not go to the local pub quiz? There are many places you can go to combine your interests and meeting other people, you just need to think outside of the box.

If you want to meet people generally, there are countless places you can start to go for yourself and socialize with new people. The more you do this, the more confident you'll feel at striking up conversations and trying to build up a rapport. It's far easier to find people than you might think. Let's look at a few potential spots.

- Coffee shops
- Bars
- Public transport/bus stops
- Volunteering centers or whilst doing charity work/fundraising
- Local meetups advertised online
- Whilst walking the dog in the park
- Gym
- Museums and art galleries
- Parties and family gatherings
- Sports and fitness classes, e.g. yoga, dance classes, etc.
- Evening or weekend classes
- Pub quizzes
- Sporting events
- Weddings
- Joining a sports team
- Workplace
- Religious groups
- Wine clubs/book clubs, etc.
- Music festivals.

The list goes on. By choosing something that actually interests you, you're more likely to meet people with whom you have common ground. That means it will be easier to build up a rapport from the start and you won't need to work quite so hard.

THE HABITS OF PEOPLE WHO CAN EASILY MAKE FRIENDS

Some people find it very easy to meet new people and strike up a friendship. The best way to emulate their efforts is to find out what their habits are and to start incorporating them into your own life. You can start working on these habits right now!

Be Your Own Best Friend First

You can't expect other people to want to spend time with you and genuinely like you if you don't really like yourself much. You need to work on your relationship with yourself before you try and make friendships with others. Many people are scared of spending time alone, but this is actually one of the most nourishing things you can do. It's not about being lonely, it's about choosing to spend time in your own company.

This means you're more self-assured, you don't need the company of others and instead, you want it, which is altogether different.

So, how can you work on your relationship with yourself? Nourish your soul, do things you really enjoy, give yourself compliments, keep a list of your positive traits and add a new one to it every day, learn more about who you are and what makes you tick, and don't be afraid to do things on your own, such as going to the movies or going out for dinner. The more assured you are in your own company, the better company you'll be for others.

Focus on Experiences

Friendly people don't chase people for the sake of it, they focus upon the experience. This means they target where they spend their time and as a result, they meet people with who they're likely to get on well with.

In our last section, I talked about where you should go to meet new people and that if you want to meet people with whom you share common ground, you should go to places that bring you joy and interest first and foremost. This is what friendly people do; not to meet people, but to enjoy an experience. Meeting people is a pleasant side effect.

You'll be far more relaxed and, in your element, when you're in a location that you enjoy or doing an activity that brings you happiness. That makes you a better version of yourself and someone who others will want to connect with.

Be Positive

Positive people radiate joy and they're far more approachable too. Would you rather spend time around someone who is upbeat or someone who is more akin to Eeyore from Winnie The Pooh? People will go for the Tigger character time after time.

Developing a positive attitude will bring many benefits into your life, not least in helping you become a more comfortably sociable person.

Positivity radiates from you and it will make you more approachable, it will naturally make you smile more, and these are all qualities and elements which make a person friendlier and more likely to strike up friendships with new people.

Start Saying 'Yes'

Do you often say 'no' when you're invited out somewhere or when a new opportunity comes your way? It's time to start saying 'yes'. You need to start pushing yourself a little and moving beyond that little zone that is so comfortable to you. If you want to meet new people, you have to go where they're likely to be and they're certainly not going to be in your living room!

Whether you're fearful of trying something new or going out when you really don't want to, push yourself to do so and you'll be far more likely to meet people who may become your new best friends.

DON'T BE AFRAID TO TAKE THE FIRST STEP!

A particular habit of friendly people is the ability and willingness to take the first step and be the one to break the ice. Terrifying? The first few times, yes, but after that, it becomes surprisingly easy.

Someone has to be the one to take that first step otherwise nothing will happen. There will be zero conversations, and zero friendships as a result of those conversations. In some situations, another person might be the one to take that first step, but in many situations, it is going to have to be you.

When you're a child, making friends is much easier. You're thrown together into a school situation and you form a bond. You might also bond over how much you like someone's toy or their hair, and it's as simple as that. It's easy to assume that building friendships when you're an adult is much harder, but the mechanics are actually the same as when you first went to kindergarten! The only difference is that you have many years of life that have forced you to build up walls around you, fears, and worries. Those are the things that hold you back and stop you from using your social skills to go out there and meet new people.

It's time to tap into the spirit of the young child you used to be and take that first step.

A little earlier I mentioned that giving someone a compliment is a great way to break the ice and start a conversation but how do you actually get to that point and prepare for it? You don't want to open your mouth and your voice comes out quivering with fear! Preparation is key.

- **Don't prepare for rejection** – The fear of being rejected will stop you from reaching out to people and taking the first step. So, rather than preparing for rejection, prepare for being accepted instead. Assume that this person is going to like you, because why wouldn't they? There is nothing wrong with you, you're wonderful!
- **Forget what happens in the movies** – In the movies, friendships are drawn together by destiny but in real life, most friendships need a little work. Know that it's not going

to fall into your lap and prepare for the need to take that first step before doing it. Take a deep breath!

- **Remember that you have nothing to lose** – You have everything to gain, however. Trying to build up a connection with someone isn't a negative thing and there is nothing you could say or do which would cause anyone to think otherwise. Of course, you need to make sure that you make a positive impression and say the right things, but we've already covered how to do that. Throw away any thoughts that cause you to think everything hinges on this conversation – it doesn't, it's just a chat.

- **Prepare to keep doing what you're doing** – Once you've made the first move and build up a connection with someone, a friendship isn't going to happen overnight. You're going to need to keep showing up to the place you met the person, keep that connection burning and growing. It takes work, but it's worth it.

- **Learn to be yourself** – For some people, making the first move is terrifying so they pretend to be someone they're not, in order to put on a mask of sorts. Doing that might get you through that first meeting but the person you're speaking to isn't getting to know the real you. It's also exhausting trying to be someone you're not and you're just not being genuine. Just be yourself. You're wonderful and you need to keep telling yourself that.

Unfortunately, breaking the ice, initiating the conversation, making the first move, whatever you want to call it, really does come down to taking a deep breath and just going for it.

NOT EVERYONE IS ON THE SAME PATH, SO MOVE ON

Before we end this chapter on making friends, it's important to mention one thing.

Not everyone you meet is going to be someone you connect with or even want to connect with after speaking to them for a few minutes. It's not possible to get along well with everyone in life and there are always going to be people who we just don't 'get'. That's fine, in fact, it's perfectly normal and happens to everyone. Don't think that you've failed somehow or your attempts to build up a conversation didn't work. It's simply that the two of you aren't meant to be friends and you have your own separate paths to walk on.

Focus on the positives from the situation, such as the fact that you took the initiative, you learned something new, you realized that you didn't want to be friends with this person and therefore, save yourself some time. Whatever the positive is, take it.

It might also be that someone doesn't want to be friends with you.

Rejection stings but it's inevitable in life sometimes. You have no idea what that person's reason for not wanting to be friends with you is and you really don't need to know. As long as you've done nothing wrong, i.e. you've not hurt or upset them in any way, just move on and find someone else who is worthy of your time.

It could be that they know someone you're close to and they don't want to blur the lines, it could be that they just don't vibe with you, and that's okay too.

The saying that "friends are the family we choose for ourselves" is true. If someone doesn't want to be friends with you or rejects you in some way, that's no reflection on you and it's simply something to shrug off and move on. I'm not saying it doesn't feel like you've been kicked, because it does; nobody likes to be rejected, but then you're not going to be everyone's cup of tea.

If everyone in the world got along with everyone else, it just wouldn't work. It sounds like it would be idyllic but in reality, it would be a mess. We're supposed to be close to people who we vibe with, who we have common ground with, and who we build a rapport with. It's not possible to get along with everyone because sometimes our differences in the opinion just don't gel.

If you're rejected by someone in this way, be kind to yourself. Know that you did nothing wrong, that it's not a reflection on your character, and instead hold your true friends closer to you and invest more time in them. Also, take heart in the fact that you tried to build up a friendship with someone new, using your social skills, and that shows true progress on your journey to mastering communication.

CHAPTER THOUGHTS

Friends make life better, that's a fact. However, not everyone finds it easy to go out and meet new people who may become friends. The good news is that you can practice and learn. Whilst you may never build up the rapport that Monica, Chandler, Joey, et al had, you will be able to create connections with people who enjoy the same things as you.

Be brave and make that first move, know that everyone else is probably worried about taking the first step and breaking the ice too, and simply get out there and enjoy yourself. By doing so, you'll find that people gravitate towards you naturally, because you seem like a happy and upbeat person.

8

GOING BEYOND BASIC SMALL TALK BY NOT RUNNING OUT OF THINGS TO SAY

When it comes to starting conversations with new people, one thing which strikes fear into the hearts of most people is running out of things to say.

It's awkward. You stand or sit there, no idea what to say, your mind goes blank, the other person is also floundering, not sure what to say or do, and you want the ground to open up and swallow you.

I've been in this situation a few times, but you know what? I'm still here. I survived and nothing terrible happened, and you'll survive too.

In this chapter I'm going to talk about why resorting to small talk isn't just filler or fluff, and why it can sometimes be a great way to turn the heat down on a difficult conversation or pass a little time whilst inspiration strikes you for conversation topics once more. I'm also going to give you a few ideas to use during your conversations, so you never actually run out of things to say, you might just need a minute to remember them!

STARTING WITH SMALL TALK ISN'T WRONG

There is a view that small talk isn't worthwhile. I disagree. Small talk isn't just filler, it's a way to find out more about a person, to ask questions, and to delve a little deeper. By doing that, you build up your confidence and you avoid jumping in too quickly to deep conversations. Small talk helps you to find that all-important common ground we were talking about earlier; you can't just walk over to someone and ask them what they have in common with you, you need to be more subtle than that!

Small talk is a very valuable tool to help you build rapport and whilst most people don't enjoy it, assuming that it's pointless, turning your attention away from that viewpoint and realizing that it's useful, may help you to engage in general banter more easily.

Of course, when you experience one of those momentary pauses in conversation, small talk can be your savior. This helps you to avoid the conversation ending prematurely or awkwardly – who said small talk wasn't worthwhile?

Small talk should cover general topics and not delve too deeply into specific areas or controversial subjects. I'm talking about things like the weather, a big entertainment new story, the upcoming holidays, sports, or lighthearted current events. You can usually rely upon such things. For instance, "did you see the Oscars last night? Some of those dresses were amazing!" Or, "I watched the game with my partner last night, are you into sports?"

As you can see, small talk deflects the attention away from anything too deep but allows the conversation to keep going, therefore, slowly building up that rapport.

Small talk can also be about what is going on around you, such as if you're both standing at a bus stop and a car drives by far too fast, or it suddenly rains very fast and catches everyone out.

In a work situation, small talk doesn't have to be about the actual job, but can be about things which connect you as colleagues, e.g. "Jenny thanks so much for making those cookies in the canteen, they're fantastic" or "what are everyone's plans for the weekend?"

Small talk is something you should try to see as a positive tool to help you build up conversations and rapport, rather than something which makes you cringe on the inside.

TURN YOUR FILTER DOWN A NOTCH

Everyone has a filter, but the fact that you're struggling to socialize means that maybe your filter is turned up just a little too high.

Your filter is in the internal voice that tells you not to say something because it's inappropriate, people won't like it, or maybe people will laugh at you. Through every single day, we have countless thoughts, a running inner dialogue that we use to talk to ourselves and wrestle with ideas and feelings. When you have no filter, it basically means that every single thought or idea that comes into your mind also comes out of your mouth. You basically don't screen anything that you say.

This is good and bad in equal measures.

Not thinking before you speak isn't to be recommended. You may say something which offends someone, you may say something which really isn't appropriate, or you might wish you'd just kept your mouth closed! However, having your filter turned up too high is equally as damaging.

By keeping your filter up, you're not allowing yourself to come up with free conversation topics. You're too stilted, too controlled. Some of your thoughts and ideas will be fantastic conversation starters and filler, it's just that you need to weed out the inappropriate or strange ones and use the good ones instead.

Holding yourself back from having a conversation isn't going to help you build your social skills and you're basically standing in your own way. It's better to allow your filter to be set to medium instead. Don't be afraid to allow your inner dialogue out, but screen it a little before it leaves your mouth.

YOUR INTERESTS WILL COME IN HANDY

If you're struggling with conversation topics, lean upon something which is familiar to you, such as your interests. Those will never let you down and the passion you have for them will show through to the person you're speaking with. It's even more useful if they share the same interest as you, or maybe they're keen to learn more about them.

Most people enjoy watching movies, reading, or walking in nature, so those are pretty safe topics, but if you have a different or unusual hobby/pastime, don't be afraid to talk about it. The other person will be interested in what you do and how you do it, and maybe they might decide to take it up for themselves!

When talking about your hobbies, however, don't downplay them. A lot of the time, people who struggle with social skills tend to play down anything in their life which is positive. I know I used to. I had quite a self-deprecating attitude and sense of self and this meant that I found it especially hard to take compliments. Thankfully, as my confidence has grown, this has changed, but back in the day, I was quite keen to play down anything that I was interested in or which I was good at. I guess this was because I was scared of being laughed at or that the other person wouldn't find it as interesting as me.

However, I've come to learn that's not the point of having hobbies. If you enjoy something, why hide it? Talk about it and share it with the other person. Share a little and see how they respond, and when they ask questions, answer them in-depth, asking them questions about their hobbies to bring them into the conversation too.

Hobbies can be a great way to reignite a conversation that might be starting to stilt a little or to actually start a conversation in the first place. It doesn't always have to be about the weather!

TALK ABOUT WHAT'S IN THE CURRENT NEWS

A little earlier I mentioned that it's best to avoid any subjects which are particularly sensitive, e.g. politics or religion, and I also mentioned big news stories in that too. However, if the news story isn't too problematic to talk about, e.g. it's not about something which is going to upset the other person, current news events are good ways to get a conversation started and to keep it rolling on.

There are a few things you need to remember when using news stories as conversation starters, however. Not everyone has the same opinion as you, and the news is, for the most part, multi-dimensional. For instance, if you talk about the US Presidential election, you could find that you're speaking to someone who is rooting for the other guy when you're firmly in the opposite camp. Most people find this easy to navigate, but you might be speaking to someone who is extremely passionate about this topic and as a result, their heckles rise, rather than allowing a rapport to be built.

The most important thing to remember here is that if you do experience views about certain issues that are quite strong, don't judge or push them down. The other person is allowed their opinions and views just as much as you are and by belittling them or showing the other person that you're not taking their view seriously, you're putting yourself on track towards a very negative first impression, one that may never be overcome.

Hear the other person out, let them talk about their view, nod along and show that you're listening, and be as open-minded as you can be. Remember, we can't all be the same, we can't all think and believe the same things. That's what makes life and humans so wonderful – we're a huge melting pot of differences that are as equally wonderful as one another. Judging someone for having a different view to you is closed-minded and that's a pretty negative trait. You never know, by listening to someone's view on a particular subject, you might learn something, or your own view might be changed too.

For the most part, however, when talking about current news events, it's probably best to stick to "safe" subjects. If there was an earthquake, a volcano eruption, or an adverse weather event, these are subjects that can be spoken about quite safely and you can both empathize with those involved.

Celebrity and entertainment news can also prove to be a safe subject or anything which doesn't lead towards a passionate discussion. However, you shouldn't automatically steer clear of passionate discussion because that could be the one thing that bonds you together and creates that future friendship. Always remember, however - if you need to, agree to disagree.

EVER HEARD OF THE SNOWBALL TECHNIQUE?

A good way to make sure that you never run out of things to say is to use the snowball technique.

The idea for this technique comes from a small topic which is rolled around, opinions and views added to it by various people, until it becomes a bigger conversation, involving several people or opening up both parties to expressing more opinions.

You can use this technique to keep the conversation going and to hold the other person's attention, without having to worry about them becoming bored or unsure of what to say themselves. You'll also learn a lot about the other person by using this technique, which will help you to look for common ground and hopefully build up a rapport.

Step 1 – Ask a question but wrap it in something less obvious

You need to start the technique by asking a question, but you don't want them to feel like you're interviewing them. To do that, surround the question in an observation to make it more conversational, such as "I work in the hospital too, which department do you work in?"

Step 2 – Make sure you listen carefully

Show the other person that you're listening by making eye contact, nodding along, and making agreeable noises, such as "uh-huh", "hmm", "oh". This is also ideal for getting the ball rolling with the conversation because it turns the attention away from you and helps you to build confidence.

Step 3 – Repeat back what you've learned but add something extra

The key is not to do this in a parrot fashion but to show the other person that you were listening and that to encourage them to carry on and move the conversation onto another topic or expand on the current one. The best way to do this is to give your opinion on what they've just said. "oh, you work in the x-ray department, I bet that's really interesting. How long have you worked there?"

Step 4 – Repeat the above step

The idea is to keep adding something else to the conversation and digging into it a little more deeply. So, when they tell you how long they've worked in the x-ray department, you could add another detail and then another question. "My friend used to work in the x-ray department at another hospital, they really enjoyed it, do you like it?" This also has the added bonus of helping them to open up a little more which helps you to find out whether there is that all-important common ground to build up a rapport.

Step 5 – Remember an earlier detail

The idea isn't just to keep the conversation flowing, but to ensure it's authentic and that the other person knows that you're paying attention. A good way to do that is to remember something they said earlier and use it to take the conversation even further. "You've worked in the x-ray department for six years, that's a long time! What did you do before that?"

As you can see, the conversation grows in momentum, just like a snowball rolling down a hill. The hope is that as you ask questions, they open up more to you and they also ask you questions that allow the conversation to become multi-faceted. This is a great technique to use because it gives you a general structure to follow and allows you to feel confident in the fact that you're not going to run out of things to say.

CHAPTER THOUGHTS

One of the biggest worries for people who lack social skills is that if they do strike up a conversation, they're going to run out of things to say. There are a million things to talk about, it's simply that they're evading you in the moment because you're nervous. Relax and allow yourself to use your interests or news events to strike up small talk. The idea that small talk is useless is completely wrong. It allows you to search for that all-important common ground.

Also practice using the snowball technique, even if you have to practice in the mirror to begin with. This is a great and structured way to build up the momentum of a conversation and give you more confidence to keep going too.

9

TALKING ISN'T EVERYTHING – LEARNING TO BECOME AN EFFECTIVE LISTENER

Think back to our first chapter when I explained in detail about emotional intelligence (EQ). Can you remember the elements that make up EQ? One of those was listening.

A huge part of communication has nothing to do with what you say and everything to do with how you present yourself to the other person. In addition, it's also about how you understand them, via reading their body language and also listening to what they're saying and what they're not saying.

For instance, if they're talking fast and appear a little flustered, would that tell you that they're nervous? Or maybe they're lying? If someone is fidgeting, avoiding eye contact, and stumbling over their words, what would that tell you? These are all ways you can really build up a picture of what is really going on and therefore learn to communicate in a far more effective way.

In this chapter, we're going to focus on the art of listening. You might think listening is super-easy; you literally just, well, listen. However, it's not just about hearing words, it's about putting the picture together. Not everyone says what they mean or tells you the full story. Listening will allow you to read that situation accurately. In addition, listening, and showing the other person that you're listening, will deepen the connection you're building, keep that rapport going, and help you to build up your social circle, or indeed move a little further up the ladder with your professional career.

You will get nowhere in this journey without learning how to listen. In particular, you need to learn the art of active listening. Let's explore this topic a little more.

REMEMBER, A CONVERSATION ISN'T ONE WAY

In order for a conversation to be enriching and to help you to build up a rapport, it needs to be a two-way deal. That means one person speaks whilst the other person listens, and then they swap tasks, keeping the swapping going throughout the conversation. Without this to-and-fro motion, a conversation just doesn't work.

By listening, you learn more about the person and the topic they're talking about, you build up that rapport that's so important when building connections, and you can easily find out whether you and that person have much in common.

If you search for a definition of listening, you'll find that it's more than just hearing. It's being able to understand the message someone is conveying to you with their words whilst also showing them that you're interested and paying attention. You can show you're paying attention by nodding along, by making agreeable noises, by maintaining eye contact (although not constantly, that would be nothing more than uncomfortable), and by repeating back what they've told you in a summarized version and asking questions.

These are all important steps to add to your social skills repertoire and to build up your communication level naturally.

WHY LISTENING IS SO IMPORTANT

You might wonder why listening is actually important. As long as you say the right thing at the right time and you get the general gist, surely that's enough? Not at all. People aren't stupid and they're going to get a feel if you're not paying attention. Even a glance in the opposite direction for a couple of seconds too long, an ill-timed sigh, or not quite catching the end of the sentence can tell the other person that you're far from in-tune with what they're saying. By doing that, you're not only being quite rude but you're also damaging the rapport that you might have worked hard to build up, or if it's the first time you've met them, giving them a very poor first impression of you.

Never underestimate just how important listening is and know that it goes far beyond just hearing words. Hearing is literally just that, hearing sounds, and nothing more. However, listening is hearing words, putting them together into a meaning, and interpreting how that meaning links into the rest of the information you're gathering. When you learn to become an active and effective listener, all of this is done simultaneously, within seconds, and without too much effort, but before you get to that point, you'll need to pay far more attention than you normally would.

Listening is important for many reasons:

- Quality communication is impossible without listening
- When you're effectively listening, you're showing the other person you're paying attention
- It keeps the conversation going and stops those awkward silences
- It helps you to understand the other person's point of view and therefore enhances your empathy
- It avoids misunderstandings and errors of judgment
- It helps us to connect with other people in the simplest of ways
- It helps us to pull together the real meaning of someone's words, by interpreting their non-verbal cues at the same time
- It helps you look for common ground that can help you to build up rapport and quality connections with other people
- It helps you to sort out problems and resolve issues that may be causing conflict
- It helps the other person to feel respected and understood
- It will take your career and your personal life to another level.

How many times have you been in the company of someone who just seems a little 'off'? Their body language is low, they aren't making eye contact, they seem down, and they're speaking to you in a slow and non-interested way. When you ask them what's wrong, they say "nothing, I'm fine". Do you believe them? If you're a poor listener then yes, you'll take their words at face value and you'll assume that they are indeed as fine as they say they are. However, as you learn to use active listening, you'll know that their words are being contradicted by their non-verbal cues and they're actually covering up their real emotions. When you reach that point, you'll know that your EQ level has risen because that's when you're showing real empathy.

YOUR STEP BY STEP GUIDE TO BECOMING AN EFFECTIVE LISTENER

You know why listening is important and you know that it's going to help you build up your social skills and make you a fantastic communicator, but how do you get from where you are now to being an effective listener?

Step 1 – Think of every conversation as a method of learning something

The best way to approach a conversation is with learning in mind. By thinking in this way, you'll be keener to listen and as a result, you'll find that you really tune into what is being said and how it's being said. Assume that every single person you have a conversation with has the role of a teacher in some way.

Step 2 – Slow down and stop thinking about what you're going to say next

When you're nervous about holding conversations with people you've never met before, it's easy to try and pre-empt what you're going to say next. However, by doing that you're actually hindering your efforts to listen and you're also making the whole thing appear and feel unnatural. Turn your attention towards the person who is speaking and give them your undivided attention. Push any other thoughts out of your mind.

Step 3 – Encourage dialogue with open-ended questions

You need something worthwhile to listen to and that means giving the other person a chance to speak. Encourage them by asking open-ended questions, avoiding anything which is likely to lead towards a 'yes' or 'no' answer. This is a closed-ended question and is a real conversation killer. Of course, once you ask one of these questions and the person starts to speak, tune into them completely.

Step 4 – Show the person you're listening

You need to make the other person know you're listening to them and that will keep the conversation going. You can do that by nodding along to what they're saying, mirroring their body language (more on that shortly), maintaining eye contact, and making encouraging noises sparingly, such as "uh-huh" or "mmm".

Step 5 – Give them a summary of what you heard

This doesn't only help your understanding, but it reinforces to the other person that you've listened to them. By doing this, you're also ensuring that there are no misunderstandings. You don't need to parrot everything back to them but a quick summary such as "so you went to the park because you heard the dog was on the loose?" or whatever else you understood from the conversation.

Step 6 – Be aware of your body language and facial expressions

Make sure that you're not in-avertedly doing something which might show the other person that you're not listening or that you'd rather be elsewhere. This includes pulling a strange face without realizing it or sighing at the wrong moment. I'm going to explain a lot more about body language in a later chapter but it's certainly something you need to be very aware of because it speaks volumes.

It's particularly important to be aware of your facial expressions if the person you're speaking to is talking about something which you don't agree with or which you find strange. Remember to respect the other person's point of view or opinion and be non-judgmental and open-minded. That includes showing the other person that you completely accept their view too.

5 THINGS MOST PEOPLE DO WRONG IN CONVERSATIONS, AND HOW TO LEARN FROM THEM

There are many habits and behaviors that derail a conversation and make it far less likely that a rapport will be established or that the person speaking is going to feel listened to and taken seriously. It's important to know whether you're developing any of these habits or whether you're already using them because that knowledge will help you to change your tactics and eradicate these habits from your life.

Let's look at 5 specific things that people do wrong in conversations, particularly when they're supposed to be listening. If you do notice these are things you do, pay attention to the advice on what to do instead and be more mindful when you're having conversations in the future. It's very easy to concentrate on other things when you do have a low confidence level related to your social skills but by turning your attention to the speaker, you'll be able to show them that you're listening completely.

Mistake 1 – Jumping to conclusions or making snap judgments

Let the person finish before jumping in with your view on the situation. Firstly, that means you've formed a judgment of the problem or situation and that's not something we should be doing when trying to communicate with others.

Instead, let them finish and be open-minded, remembering that everyone has their view and it's just as valid as yours. You don't have to agree with them, and you don't have to show them that you don't either.

Mistake 2 – Multi-tasking or daydreaming

If your mind isn't on what the person is saying, they're going to notice and they're going to feel pretty aggrieved that your attention isn't on them. Don't allow yourself to think about the things you need to do, or half-listen to the conversation and half-listen to the radio. Also, don't try and think about what you're going to say next either. It's understandable to do that if you're a little nervous about speaking to people you don't know, but by being distracted in this way, you're not allowing yourself to listen properly and they're going to see that.

Mistake 3 – Offering a solution

People don't always speak about things because they want advice or a solution, sometimes they're just talking and being polite. If you're always interrupting and trying to offer a solution, it means you're not showing empathy because you're not putting yourself in their shoes. Instead, you're being proactive, which is a completely different thing altogether.

You might have the best intentions at heart but it's possible that this person doesn't want your advice, they simply want to talk. If they want a solution or advice, just know that they'll ask you for it and then you're well within your rights to offer a suggestion – not before.

Mistake 4 – Interrupting

It's possible that you're excitable because you've heard something you have an experience of and you want to put your side of the story over, but interrupting is a huge no-no when someone else is speaking.

You might not be trying to end the conversation early, but it shows the other person that you're far too busy to listen and you want them to get to the point already. This isn't going to show you in the best light and it's a huge conversation killer. If you want to say something, wait until they've finished.

Mistake 5 – Changing the subject or deflecting away from the subject

Sometimes we remember something halfway through a conversation and we want to say it before we forget again. However, if you change or deflect the subject it tells the other person that you're not interested in what they were talking about and that you were bored. It might not be the case, but that's how it comes across.

If you really do want to say something which is totally unrelated to the original conversation, try and weave it in or link to it in some way. You might have to be creative, but it's better than just abruptly changing the direction of the conversation.

CHAPTER THOUGHTS

Listening is an underrated skill that can make or break your communication efforts. Even the slightest hint that you're not truly paying attention can cause someone to avoid talking to you again and can create a very poor first impression. However, by listening properly, you gain so much. Not only do you learn something new, but you also build a rapport with someone who may turn out to be someone you can socialize with, or a good professional contact.

Practice your listening skills by doing more than just hearing the words.

10

BODY LANGUAGE IS THE KEY TO SUCCESSFUL INTERACTIONS

Throughout this book so far, I've talked about body language a few times and reassured you that we're going to delve into the subject in more detail later on. Now is that time!

Body language is one of the most powerful methods of speaking you possess, and to do it, you don't even open your mouth. Being able to read the body language of other people allows you to understand them in much greater detail and it also allows you to play the role of detective in some ways too. Not everyone says exactly what they mean, but their body language will always give them away.

In this chapter, I'm going to talk about what body language is, why it's important to be able to read it and why you need to be very mindful of the type of body language you're showing to other people.

NOT EVERYTHING HAS TO BE VERBAL

Non-verbal communication is just as important as verbal and in some cases, more important. Someone can say words, but their body language can totally contradict them. I gave the example earlier of someone saying, "I'm fine", when their body language is slumped, and they won't look you in the eye. When that happens, you're more likely to believe what their body language is telling you than their words because it's so powerful.

Body language is just one type of non-verbal communication. The others include facial gestures, how you speak, whether you maintain eye contact, and hand gestures. These are all unspoken ways of communicating what we really mean and usually what we really feel.

When you're able to read body language, you get the full message and the full meaning of whatever someone is trying to tell you, or in some cases, what they're trying not to tell you. This makes you an effective communicator and it also allows you to build up a true rapport.

Someone with good levels of emotional intelligence can read non-verbal cues very quickly and tends to even get a gut feeling when something isn't quite right. This isn't a psychic ability, it's just that they're able to read signs quickly and effectively and put the picture together. That tells you just how powerful these non-verbal signs are, even more than actual verbal words. If you pit the two against each other, body language will win out every time.

USING NONVERBAL LANGUAGE TO YOUR ADVANTAGE

In your journey to become a master communicator, you have to place a huge amount of importance upon body language and being able to use these non-verbal cues to your advantage during a conversation. You can make the other person feel at ease by ensuring that your body language is soft, open, and relaxed, or you can show that you really mean business if you need to, by sitting upright and appearing professional.

Once you understand body language a little better, you can use it to show your intentions and make sure that the other person doesn't get the wrong impression of you. It also helps you to show others that you're listening to them, and it stops you from being misunderstood and misread.

The other plus point is that when you understand body language, you can read it and use it to think of interesting things to say. Body language can guide the conversation in some ways because it gives you cues about the underlying emotions of the person you're speaking to. You can use this to show empathy, to help them out even, and to encourage them to open up.

All you need to do is know what good body language looks like, versus the bad. Handily, that's something we're going to explore in our next couple of sections.

IT'S ALL GOOD: THE POSITIVE NONVERBAL CUES

In order to start working towards using positive nonverbal cues, and kicking out some of the negative ones, you need to be more aware of the body language you're showing to those around you. This is going to be quite time consuming at first because it's possible you have no idea that you're showing a poor or maybe positive example to the world.

Simply be more mindful of what you do when you're communicating, how you show yourself, what your face is doing, what your hands are doing, and how you're standing. Over time, positive body language will become a thing of habit.

Let's look at some examples of positive non-verbal communication and how you can start to weave these naturally into your socializing efforts.

- **Tilting your head to one side** – This is a very slight inflection to one side whilst someone is talking and it shows not only that you're listening, but that you're also very interested in what they have to say. However, do make sure that you don't squint your eyes or pull a face at the same time, as this could show that you don't believe them or you're not taking them seriously. Keep your face neutral, or simply raise your eyebrows in interest.
- **Quickly rubbing your hands together** – You might think this means that you're cold, but that's not the only reason! Depending upon the context, you can use this non-

verbal cue to show that you're excited or keen to do something or speak about something. It's usually accompanied by a smile to get the right meaning across.

- **Sitting with your palms facing up** – Obviously to do this your hands also need to be open and it's the same kind of thing you would do if you were worshipping at a church. In that situation, you're showing respect to God, but in a communicative situation, you're showing that you're being open and honest. This is a good move to try and build trust.

- **Sitting up straight with your shoulders pulled back** – Be careful that you're not sitting bolt upright here; the stance should be straight but relaxed and the idea is that your shoulders pulled back means you're not slouching. This shows that you're relaxed and professional at the same time. You can also practice this as you're walking too, as it shows that you're relaxed within yourself and confident.

- **Rubbing your chin** – This shows that you're interested. Think about Sherlock Holmes when he was thinking about a case and trying to solve it – that's the look you're going for! This type of body language is usually shown when someone is trying to think and decide on something, but it can also show that you're deep in thought.

- **Mirroring their body language** – You might find that you do this without thinking because most of us do when we're with someone we're talking to and we're interested, or someone we feel comfortable with. If you're mirroring someone's body language it means that you're basically copying how they're standing. So, if they're leaning against a wall, you will do the same subconsciously. It shows that you're relaxed, but it has to be done naturally otherwise it comes over as false.

- **Gently leaning into the person** – If you're speaking to someone, lean into them very slightly to show that you're listening. Be careful not to lean in too much as this could be misconstrued, but a slight lean shows that they have your attention and your interest.

- **Maintaining eye contact** – Be careful not to stare them out, but holding someone's eye contact and being relaxed within it shows that you're listening to them, you're interested and you're comfortable. Remember to blink and look away for a couple of seconds occasionally.

- **Nodding along** – Nodding your head whilst someone is speaking shows that you're listening but also shows that you're agreeing with what they're saying. This can encourage them to carry on speaking, especially if you throw in a few "uh-huh" or "hmm" noises too.

WARNING! NEGATIVE CUES TO WATCH OUT FOR

We've talked about positive non-verbal communication and now we need to cover the negative side of things. Remember that body language happens without much thought, it's totally subconscious and it can be interpreted in different ways according to the person you're conversing with.

However, if you're speaking to someone and you see some of these negative points, it could show you that they're feeling uncomfortable or maybe not interested in what you're saying. In that case, you can adjust your conversation or simply change the topic completely. You should also be mindful that you're not showing these non-verbal cues yourself.

- **Crossing arms over the chest** – Crossed arms show defensiveness because they act as a barrier between you and the other person. It can also show that the person is displeased with the topic or that they don't agree.
- **Biting your nails** – For many people, nail-biting is a habit that is born out of nerves or stress, but it can also show that you're not interested in what someone is saying, and you're distracted. Even if it is out of nerves, you're showing the other person that they make you nervous and this could be a huge barrier to communication and rapport.
- **Furrowed brow** – This is a sign that someone is confused or they're simply not paying attention and their mind is elsewhere. If a furrowed brow is accompanied by a hand on the cheek, it can show that you're lost in thought and you've totally lost the flow of the conversation. Either way, it's a barrier you don't need.
- **Tapping fingers or tapping a pen** – Tapping something means that you're impatient and you'd rather be elsewhere. It shows that you're bored and would much rather end this conversation quickly. Of course, it can also be nerves but it's not often interpreted that way.
- **Touching the nose** – This isn't an obvious one but touching your nose can show the other person that you're

lying because it's a form of fidgeting. It can also be that you don't believe them or that you're feeling rejected.

- **Forming a tent with your fingers, or placing the tips of your fingers together** – This is a way of telling the other person that you feel superior to them or that you're in authority. It's a quick way to form a huge communication barrier and stop the other person from communicating any further.

- **Crossing your legs at the knee or ankle** – This is another form of defensiveness because it's that barrier you form between you and the other person once more. You might think it's comfortable or even demure, but it can show that you're lying, you're worried, you're nervous, or that you'd just rather be elsewhere.

- **Sitting too close to the edge of your chair** – This doesn't show that you're super-excited to hear what someone is going to say, instead it shows that you're very nervous and you're trying to make a quick getaway.

- **Putting your head in your hands** – Even if you do this for just a second, it shows that you're bored and frustrated. It might also show that you're embarrassed or ashamed of something.

- **Playing with your hairs, rings, or clothing** – Any type of fidgeting is pretty negative and shows that you're either nervous, you're bored, you're impatient, or you're feeling insecure.

YOU GIVE THEM OFF TOO ...

Everyone has body language, but you might not be aware of your own. In order to be able to use more of the positive non-verbal cues and less of the negative ones, you need to build up awareness. How can you do that?

It really comes down to being mindful of your actions during a conversation, but you could ask a trusted friend or family member to highlight any common habits that you use when you're talking. Maybe you slouch a lot, or perhaps you fidget without realizing it. The problem with body language is that it's completely subconscious, so you're not even thinking about it. For the most part, you don't even know what you're doing.

Being aware means that you can change your habits and make the positive ones your default setting. You could even try having pretend conversations with others in a full-length mirror. Practice using positive body language cues and watch how it changes your entire look and how you could be perceived by other people. The more you do this, the more aware you'll be of your body language when you're in real conversations and you'll be able to spot any negative habits quickly and reverse them.

CHAPTER THOUGHTS

Body language is extremely powerful, and it has the potential to completely change someone's words into a different meaning altogether. When you show negative non-verbal traits to the world, you're telling them a story that perhaps you don't mean to tell. It could show people that you're not listening, you're not interested, and you'd really rather be anywhere else but there. You probably don't mean that, but that's what you're telling them, and they have no reason to believe anything else.

By learning more about positive and negative body language, and by practicing being more aware of your own, you can ensure that you're showing the best possible version of yourself to other people. In addition, you can start to recognize body language in other people and use it to your own advantage when you're socializing.

11

MAKE AWKWARD SILENCES YOUR BEST FRIEND & EFFORTLESSLY MOVE PAST THEM UNAFFECTED

THE DREADED AWKWARD SILENCE.

Even some of the most comfortable communicators in the world seem to think that a momentarily lull in the conversation has to add up to a major disaster. It doesn't.

As you build up your social skills and start to branch out more in terms of communicating with other people, you have to be prepared for an awkward silence or two. You also need to change your view regarding these silences and see them as just a part of the deal, and not necessarily a negative event.

Many people blame themselves when an awkward silence happens, thinking that maybe they said the wrong thing, or they weren't exciting enough. However, sometimes these silences need to happen as part of a naturally evolving conversation. It could be that the topic has come to a natural end and both people need to think of a natural change of topic direction, or that someone has said something really interesting and even proud, and maybe it needs a moment to be digested. It could even be that one half of the conversation is feeling a little tired or distracted, and a silence has happened for a couple of seconds as a result.

Awkward silences aren't always negative and they're not always awkward either!

In this chapter, I'm going to talk about these so-called dreaded events, try to dispel the fear, and give you plenty of tools to help you deal with them when they do crop up.

THE SILENCE IS NOBODY'S FAULT

There are two common reactions to a silence – either panic or a need to quickly fill the silence with another conversation. Neither are necessary.

Silences are a natural part of a conversation and they're either an opportunity to end the conversation and move on or a chance to pause and readjust.

Firstly, you need to accept this as a fact and stop assuming that it's your fault alone when a silence does occur. You should also stop calling them 'awkward silences' because by labeling them in that way, you're creating a stigma and fear around them. Silence is normal and, in some ways, it's to be welcomed – a constantly flowing conversation sounds great but in reality, it's exhausting! Sometimes you need a second to gather your thoughts.

You should also know that the look on the other person's face isn't an expression of disappointment. They're not thinking "what is wrong with this person? They can't even hold a conversation", they're simply trying to come up with something to say themselves. Nobody likes these silences, but it's a stigma that needs to be broken down if you want to become a better communicator and if you want to get over your fear of socializing with new people. Silences are part of the deal. They are going to happen sometimes, and it doesn't mean that you're not a good fit, that there is no rapport, or that you've failed, it's just a natural part of socializing.

BE THE MORE CONFIDENT ONE

You might not be aware, but allowing a silence to become awkward is actually a choice you make. Silence isn't awkward naturally or by definition, it's just a lull in a conversation or a period of time when there is no speech from either person. There is nothing necessarily awkward about that unless you make it so.

Everyone experiences silence in conversations, and from this point, I'm going to stop labeling them as 'awkward' because they don't need to be. You will always believe them to be awkward until you realize something really quite important. You realize that you're to blame for making it awkward.

There will normally be one person within the conversation who is more confident than the other yet when a silence happens, each party blames themselves for the lull. Their minds are working super-fast to try and think of something to say, anything to rescue themselves from the cringe-worthy feel of the moment. However, in reality, both parties aren't to blame, only one is – the one who deems it awkward. If you both simply let the silence happen and accept it as a normal part of communication, it will pass, nobody will feel like they want the ground to open up and swallow them whole, and the conversation will either naturally end, or you'll come up with something else to say.

By acting the one in the conversation who is more confident, you're guiding the other person. Confidence really is a 'fake it until you make it' kind of deal and if you act confident, sooner or later you'll start to feel it. You'll also trick the other person into thinking that you are too and it's infectious. By going into every conversation with this confidence and understanding that silence doesn't have to be so awkward, you'll be able to side-step these moments of peril and navigate your way seamlessly through.

HOW TO GET PAST IT: BRING THE CONVERSATION BACK

If you're really keen to get the conversation back on track, you'll need a few tricks in your armory to employ whenever one of these silences takes hold. Thankfully, it's not particularly difficult to get a conversation going again, but maybe you don't actually want to continue. Think of that for a second. Maybe the conversation has come to a natural conclusion and it's time to go about your day.

In that case, all you need to do is make your excuses. "I can't believe how fast today's gone, I better get on" is enough to let the other person know that you're not at all uncomfortable with the silence but you're ready to move past it. Every conversation has to end at some point otherwise we'd all be stuck chatting forever!

If you want to revitalize a conversation that seems to have been stilted by silence, here are a few tricks you can use.

- Turn the conversation towards a story on the news
- Observe something happening around you, such as a big gust of wind or asking them where they got their pretty necklace from
- Share a highlight of your day to get the conversation moving again
- Recall something that you spoke about earlier in the conversation and turn the conversation back around to it
- Mention something that you're really looking forward to, e.g. "I can't wait for dinner, I'm cooking a huge roast"
- Ask open-ended questions rather than questions that require a 'yes' or a 'no' answer
- If all else fails, point out the silence and make a joke about it. This will take the sting from it and help the other person to feel relaxed.

Getting a conversation back on track doesn't need to be a big thing. You can simply ask a question and act like the silence never happened. Remember, it's only awkward if you make it so.

AWKWARD SILENCE CAN BE YOUR BEST FRIEND

You always have the choice over whether you deem something to be awkward or not. If you choose for it not to be, then it won't be. It's really that simple.

Even when you're not conversing verbally, you're still using communication. Remember in our last chapter that we talked about the power of body language? During these silences, your body language will be deafening if you allow it to become negative. However, if you maintain a positive stance and use the habits I mentioned as positive, you'll show the other person that you're not concerned about this brief silence and that will allow them to relax too. By doing so, the silence will end far faster. It also shows that you're relaxed within yourself, which is a very enviable trait.

Use the silence as a second to gather your thoughts. What do you want to say to this person? What do you want to find out? Whilst you're doing this, your body language will be speaking for you, so always be mindful of it, as before.

Use the silence as a tool rather than something which causes you to kick-start into fight or flight mode. You also shouldn't feel like the pressure is entirely on you. The other person can also break the silence too!

Using this silence as a positive just means being calm, poised, and using it as a way to think. When conversations are batting back and forth it's easy to forget yourself and what you want to say. Use the conversation lull to regroup.

TAKE IT AS YOUR CUE

Of course, a silence sometimes means it's time to end the conversation and you can take it as a sign that you've done well, the conversation is over, and it's time to bid them goodbye. This doesn't have to be done in a stilted, "okay, we've run out of things to say" kind of way, it can be a natural end.

Sometimes a silence happens because you literally have run out of things to say but not negatively because the conversation has exhausted itself. There is literally nothing left to say about that topic, and you don't always have to find a way to fill a silence either. It's a choice of what you want to do, and you shouldn't feel pressure to quickly come up with an interesting new topic.

As I mentioned earlier, simply let the other person know that you're finished talking now. It sounds harsh, but it doesn't have to be! "I suppose I'd better get back to work" accompanied by a good-natured shrug and a smile is enough to end the chat in a positive way. "It's been really nice to talk to you. I've got to get on because my bus is due, but we must meet up again". These are examples that allow you to signal an end to the conversation but leaving it on a positive and upbeat note.

Don't always feel the need to fill the silence, sometimes silence is a cue.

CHAPTER THOUGHTS

We're quick to label silences as awkward, but what about the saying "silence is golden"? It's a truth and one you must embrace.

You choose whether a silence becomes awkward or whether it simply means a lull. Nobody can speak constantly for the full course of a conversation, no matter how long or short it is. We have to give ourselves time to think and breathe occasionally!

Silences are nobody's fault, they're completely natural, but it is your fault if you choose to make it an awkward moment.

You get to choose whether the conversation is over or whether you want to continue it on, but learning how to use these lulls to your own advantage is key if you want to overcome your fear of these moments of silence and continue your journey towards increased communication mastery.

12

IT HAS ENDED – WRAPPING UP YOUR CONVERSATION

A ll conversations must come to an end.

In our last chapter, we talked about awkward silences and how these sometimes signal the end of a conversation. However, conversations don't always end with a lull or a silence, they sometimes need to be ended for another reason.

Maybe the conversation is just going round and round in circles, maybe the time is really getting on and you need to go, or maybe you're just ready to bid them goodbye. Either way, knowing how to end a conversation in a polite way and how to ensure that the conversation isn't your last, is key.

In this chapter, I'm going to talk about those very subjects. For some people, ending a conversation is difficult because they feel like they're being rude if they say, "I'm sorry but I've really got to go now", but if you don't do something, you could be standing there all day long!

Thankfully, it's not that hard to learn how to end conversations without feeling like you've just offended someone.

THE TIME HAS COME

Knowing when it's time to end a conversation is key. Allowing a conversation to go on for too long can take a good chat into bad chat territory. What starts off well starts to become stilted, you answer with monosyllabic noises and body language has started to tell you that the other person has had enough.

It's good practice to spot the signs so that you can end the chat in a friendly way and then swap details so that you can perhaps meet up again in the future. If you allow the conversation to go on for too long, especially if it's the first time you've had a conversation with someone, you might be remembered as "that one person who went on, and on, and on" and they're going to avoid wanting to talk to you again. Of course, that might seem unfair if you were pretty keen to end the conversation as well, but if you didn't show them that, how can you expect them to know? They're not mind readers!

So, what are the signs that it's time for a conversation to end?

- You're the one doing all the conversing and they're simply answering you back with 'just enough' to be polite
- You're hearing more and more monosyllabic answers, e.g. words with just one syllable, such as 'yes', 'no', 'oh', 'ah', 'okay', etc.

- The other person is avoiding eye contact, or they're starting to fidget or look around the room
- The other person yawns, glances at the clock, or looks at their watch
- Stretching
- If the other person suddenly stands up. In that case, it's a cue that they're ready to go
- They say that they better get on with work or they have to be somewhere else
- The conversation just feels heavier and harder work.

In these situations, it's time to end the conversation and go about your day. It might also be that you're the one who needs to end the conversation because you need to be somewhere perhaps. In that case, don't feel guilty – everyone has a life outside of the conversation they're currently having!

If someone is showing you signs that they want to end the conversation, be sure to notice them and take action. Dragging on a conversation is not a good idea, but you shouldn't be offended by their actions either. They may genuinely need to be somewhere, just as you may need to be too.

ANOTHER PERSON CAN HELP YOU

If you really need to end a conversation but the other person doesn't seem to be of the same opinion, how are you supposed to extract yourself politely?

You could be direct and explain that you really need to be somewhere, or you could employ a very useful tactic - bringing another person into the conversation. This tactic does rely on another person you know being close by but it's a good option to have in your mind, in case the situation does arise.

This is a very useful way to end a conversation with someone whom you don't really want to leave on their own. Maybe they look lonely or they're simply standing alone, and you feel bad to leave them there. In that case, introduce another person into the chat, stick around for a few minutes, making idle chat, and excuse yourself, leaving the other two to continue their conversation.

There are two plus points to this tactic. Firstly, you can get away from the conversation without causing offense or upset to the other person. Secondly, you can help the other two people to create a rapport and connection alongside the one you've just created. You're basically helping them out whilst helping yourself out, which is never a bad tactic to use!

It goes a little like this.

"Adam, you've been on holiday to Spain before haven't you?" Adam will say that yes, he has. "Karen here is looking to go this summer, where was it that you went?"

By doing this, you've introduced Adam into the conversation and they're talking about something which is easy-going and relevant to both parties. In that case, they've got something in common and could go on to form a rapport. You should stick around for a short while, ensuring that they keep chatting and put your input into the conversation a little too. "I'd really like to go to Spain too, I might look for this year".

Then, after a couple of minutes, you could look at your watch and say "I can't believe the time. I'm so sorry, I'm going to have to rush off and pick up the kids. Let me know where you decide to go in Spain". Then, you leave Karen chatting to Adam about Spain and you're free to go about the rest of your day.

Easy!

ENDING IT ON A GOOD NOTE

It goes without saying that you should always try to end conversations on a good note. In some ways, last impressions are as powerful as first impressions to a degree. The way you leave a person stays with them too, so you need to be sure that you end the conversation in a way that is polite, not abrupt, and that hopefully leaves them wanting to have further conversations with you in the future.

You could say something like "I'm really going to have to go in a minute but before I do, I want to tell you about this place I went to for dinner last week". That shows the other person that a) you're about to go so the conversation is coming to a natural end, but that b) you want to tell them something else first and you're keen to continue talking to them another time.

Some things to avoid include:

- Abruptly ending the conversation with "I've got to go now" and then literally just walking away
- Zero pleasantries – Always say something like "it's been great chatting to you"; avoiding this just looks rude
- Just walking away when a silence begins
- Using an excuse that is so obviously fabricated that the other person feels like you didn't enjoy talking to them

Ending on a positive note will ensure that there is a next time, and you can continue to build upon the rapport you've established.

HOW ABOUT NEXT TIME?

Assuming you want to talk to this person again, how should you go about arranging it?

Don't make them set a concrete date because that's just needy and will make them want to avoid you. However, don't be so vague that it makes them think you're just saying you want to meet up again out of politeness. You need to strike a useful piece of middle ground.

By discussing setting up a plan to meet up again it tells the other person that you had a great time talking to them and that you want to get to know them better. This can be used in a romantic situation and in a friendship situation, it works equally well regardless.

So, how can you do it without seeming too keen?

It really comes down to using your body language in the right way and choosing your words carefully. Don't allow yourself to seem desperate. By pushing your contact details onto the other person and trying to pinpoint them down to a particular date or time, you're showing that you're desperate for someone to talk to and that's not going to get you what you want.

Instead, be casual about it. You can say something like "I had a great time talking to you if you want to meet up again just let me know" and then the other person can agree, and you swap contact details. You can also agree to do something that you talked about at some point in your chat; maybe you talked about a great little coffee shop you went to and they served the best cakes or a great spot in the park for walking the dog. These ideas link back to the conversation and something you've already built up a rapport about, so they're ideal opportunities to meet up again and try and build up a deeper connection and nurture that potential new friendship.

Never just leave it cold. By doing so you're going to confuse the other person and they're not going to know whether you enjoyed the chat or not. You might not think they'll be too concerned, but you can't read their mind. How do you know they're not a little awkward in using their social skills too? Some people hide shyness or social anxiety quite well sometimes. So, don't allow an opportunity to pass and simply reach out. If they call you, great. If they don't, no problem.

CHAPTER THOUGHTS

Trying to get out of a conversation can be tricky and sometimes it's a reason why people don't want to stop and get into one in the first place! However, it doesn't always need to be difficult and you simply need to know the signs to look for that signal the conversation is naturally coming to an end.

There's no need to take offense if someone needs to be elsewhere, because there will be times you're speaking to someone and you need to go somewhere too. We all have busy lives, and we all need to expect that sometimes conversations are going to start at bad times.

Try your best to leave conversations on a positive note and swap contact numbers so you can continue to nurture the rapport you've built up. You never know, this could be a new friend to add to your growing collection!

III

KEEPING YOUR
RELATIONSHIPS AND
MAKING THEM LAST

13

HOW TO NURTURE YOUR NEWLY FORMED FRIENDSHIPS

O nce you start to create rapport with other people, you'll also start to form connections and friendships. That means all your hard work is finally paying off!

Friendships truly make life worthwhile. However, it's also worth pointing out that nothing is 100% positive all the time. Friends have arguments, conflicts, they clash on subjects, and sometimes it's painful because you don't want to argue with someone you've grown close to. However, it's important to remember that friendships are basically two human beings trying to navigate life. That means that sometimes there are going to be problems but it's about how you get through them together that counts.

As you start to build friendships, it's normal to give your all because you're worried that they're going to go away as quickly as they came. My advice is to relax and be yourself. You do not have to force things, and you have to allow friendships to develop naturally. Yes, you need to ensure that you're spending time together and you're not doing anything which causes undue upset or concern to your friend, but you also don't need to pretend to be someone you're not and you don't have to be the one always trying to reach out. Friendships are two-way deals.

This isn't meant to be a negative overview of what a friendship is by any means. Friendships are wonderful things, but when you've struggled with your social skills for a long time and then you suddenly find yourself meeting new people who want to be your friend, it can be very easy to become fearful that as quickly as you received these people into your life, they're going to be taken away. They're not.

This is something I experienced, which is why I want to highlight it to you. I battled with shyness for so long that I had very few friends. However, once I started to overcome it and open myself up to having conversations with other people, the natural thing happened – I gained more friends. It was amazing and whilst I was embracing every second, I was fearful at the same time.

By doing this, you're actually defeating the object and you're actually working against yourself. So, my advice is to relax and enjoy the fruits of your labor. You deserve this, and it's because you've worked so hard for it. However, the hard work isn't over yet!

SPENDING QUALITY TIME IS ESSENTIAL

There are many reasons why having friendships in your life is important. Not only do they make life more worthwhile and fulfilling but having friendships is actually very important for your mental health.

The benefits of having friends include:

- Helps you to feel like you belong to something other than yourself
- Helps you to identify a purpose in life
- Helps you feel happier and more positive
- Allows you to manage and reduce any stress in your life
- Boosts self-confidence
- Boosts self-worth
- Gives you a support network during difficult times, such as the loss of a loved one, relationship problems, or job issues
- Helps you to avoid unhealthy coping mechanisms during hard times
- Encourages you to talk about your feelings rather than keeping them bottled up inside.

Of course, friendships are two-way streets. For all the benefits that having friends brings to you, you should also be providing the same level of support and happiness to another person.

In order to nourish a friendship, either newly formed or long-standing, you have to put in the work and that means spending quality time together. This is a vital part of your friendship because without it, your bond will weaken and over time you'll just grow apart. Maybe this has happened to you in the past.

It's often the case when people meet early in their lives, e.g. during high school perhaps. Once they leave school, they become so engrossed with the new parts of their life that they forget to put the effort in to keep their old friendships ticking along. Before you know it, months and years have gone by and no communication has occurred. Friendships can easily die out by not dedicating quality time to one another.

You can spend time together in many different ways. This can be hanging out in person, such as going for a coffee, going for a walk, arranging to go out for a meal, etc. It can be chatting online when you don't have the time to meet up or when circumstances don't allow it. However, it's always better to limit the amount of online interaction you have and make a priority out of meeting in person or at least speaking over the phone.

The most important thing to remember is that when you do hang out together, that you're completely present in the moment. Put away your phone! Your friendships are a deeply important part of your life and by constantly being on your phone when you're supposed to be spending quality time with a friend, you're showing them that they're not that important to you.

Think how you would feel if your friend was constantly checking their phone when you were out for dinner together. You would feel annoyed, wouldn't you? And you would be right to feel that way.

Being present in the moment means ensuring that your attention is firmly on your friend and the conversation you're having. It means you can have more in-depth chats and really build upon your rapport. It also means you can share experiences together and build memories, which is what friendship is all about. If a friend is sharing a woe with you, perhaps something which has happened in their life, and you're not really in the moment or listening properly, they're going to know. Remember, your friends know you well, even if you've not been friends for that long. This means they're going to know if you're not really listening or paying attention and they're going to feel upset that you're not concerned about what they're telling you. In some cases, this can be enough to end a friendship, and that's not something you want.

By making time for your friends, making them a priority in your life, and being present in the moment when you are spending time together, you'll nourish those connections and benefit from them in a big way.

MAKING AN EFFORT HELPS TO BUILD

We've already established that to help a friendship grow and to keep it ticking along nicely, you need to spend quality time together on a regular basis. However, that also means you need to make an effort. It's vital that this effort isn't just placed on your shoulders, and equally, you shouldn't expect the other person to do all the leg work either. This is a shared responsibility.

Nurturing a friendship does take work, but whatever you put into the friendship is going to give you more out of it. You don't have to make huge gestures or plan elaborate outings; sometimes the smallest things can show that you're making an effort and that you care. For instance, sending your friend a funny meme you've found online, or maybe you see something you know they would like, so you send them a link to it. This shows them that you're thinking about them and that small action keeps things ticking along.

Small acts of kindness in friendships are so important and they really do go such a long way. Maybe you've made a cake at home and there's some leftover; when you meet up the next day, you take a piece for them to try. Perhaps you saw their favorite beverage in the supermarket, and you thought you'd surprise them. Effort doesn't always mean gifts, but it certainly always means time and attention.

However, I want to go back to the idea of being the one doing all the work for a second. This is something you need to be very mindful of. The reason is that constantly pushing could be off-putting to your friend. Maybe they're going through a stressful time at work or they're just not feeling that great at the moment. By constantly trying to get them to meet up or bombarding them with messages, you could make them feel quite stressed or annoyed.

The best advice is to invite them to do something and then leave it in their hands. You've made the effort and they will get back to you. Busy yourself with something else. If they don't reply to you, you could send a follow-up message but not straight away – leave it a few days and enquire if they're okay. That's all you need to do. Effort doesn't mean pushing too much, it means just enough to keep things moving and nourishing the connection you have.

DON'T BE AFRAID TO BE VULNERABLE

The closest and most supportive of friendships are born out of the ability to knock down walls and allow yourself to open up. That means being vulnerable.

Being vulnerable can be a terrifying experience for some people but it's important to remember that you don't have to share anything you're not comfortable with. Set yourself boundaries and work within them. You can always adjust them whenever you feel comfortable doing so.

However, on the flip side, it's also important not to be overly vulnerable and basically over-share everything that you think and feel. Your friends are there to support you, that's the truth, but they're not there to prop up your emotions and listen to every single thing that goes wrong in your life. It's about finding a happy medium.

Being vulnerable can also be difficult because someone who has been through a hard time in the past, or someone who has struggled with social skills, is likely to have built up high walls around themselves. This is especially true if someone has betrayed and hurt you in the past. However, these walls do nothing for you. You might think they're protecting you from further hurt, but in reality, they're just holding you back and stopping you from building enriching and supportive relationships with other people.

Being vulnerable means, you need to trust the other person to listen and be there for you, but this huge gamble isn't an effort wasted because it also lets your friend trust you too. Trust is a two-way deal and with friendships, it's truly a case of share and share-alike.

If you need a little nudge in the right direction, these are some of the reasons why allowing yourself to be vulnerable creates some of the best friendships around.

- Being vulnerable shows your friends that you've placed your trust in them
- Being vulnerable also encourages your friends to open up to you
- When you're vulnerable, your friends can act as encouragement for you to overcome whatever is bothering you
- When you're vulnerable it means not only that you trust your friend but also that you value honesty and openness, which are positive traits to have and show
- Friendships built on mutual sharing of worries and concerns are authentic and usually long-lasting
- Being vulnerable with your friends also gives you the confidence to go out there and solve whatever problem you're facing, because you know you have the support of your circle.

Keeping things bottled up inside is not healthy and it does nothing for your mental health. All it does is create stress and causes you to over-think. Friendships are the ideal outlet for voicing these worries, allowing your friends to listen, support, and usually advise you too. This isn't a case of judging your problem or telling you what you should do, it's about someone who knows you well, giving you their honest opinion and guiding you, should you need extra help.

Friendships without vulnerability are quite stilted and closed. You could argue that these types of friendships aren't really genuine. Yes, you know each other and enjoy spending time together but a true friendship is about sharing and supporting one another. You can't do that if you're not willing to open up and share the things that you need support in, and vice versa. Being there for one another is what takes a friendship from just two people who know each other, to two people who care about and want the best for each other.

If you struggle to open up to your new friends, perhaps because you've built those walls around you, start slowly and small. Share one detail and see how you feel. Over time, you'll feel more confident in breaking down those barriers and opening up.

THE UPS AND DOWNS OF FRIENDSHIPS

The beauty of friendship is that you're there for each other through the good and the bad. A good friend will share your sorrows and celebrate your successes and it's through these joint experiences that a true and lasting bond is formed. However, it's important to remember that in order to enrich your friendship and really be there for one another, that means showing up during the hard times in life.

It can be easy to show up for the good and only half show up for the bad. This can be because you're not sure what to say, or you feel awkward seeing your friend emotional. However, as their friend, it's your job to put that discomfort to one side and play the role you're supposed to play – supporter.

It's being there through the hard times that helps to build up a greater level of trust and as a result, your friendship will be deeper, lasting, and truly beneficial for both of you. Being there doesn't mean offering great advice or being able to understand completely, it often just means listening, running any errands they need, and being a supportive and positive figure in their life.

If you think back to the last time you went through a hard time in your life, you probably didn't really want anyone to step in and solve the problem or offer revolutionary advice, you just wanted someone to be there and to listen to you, put their arm around you and tell you that everything's going to be alright. That's the role of a friend.

There's no judgment, no telling you what to do, they're simply focused on making sure that you're doing okay and giving you a helping hand when and if you need it.

Of course, friendships aren't all about the bad times, and there has to be a balance here too. If as friends all you're doing for each other is mopping up spills and making each other feel better, it's a supportive relationship and not an actual friendship! You need to have laughs and smiles, positive memories to draw upon and those are what will power you through the hard times.

KEEPING YOUR EXPECTATIONS REALISTIC

We've been fed images of friendships since the day we were born, mostly from TV shows and blockbuster movies. Do you remember earlier, I mentioned that I always wanted a social circle akin to the one on Friends? These images can cause you to develop unrealistic expectations of your friendships, and when those expectations are inevitably not met, you become angry, worried, and it could even cause a conflict to occur between you.

It's important to remember that friends are human beings and sometimes human beings are busy with other things, tired, stressed, unwell, or simply just being a little selfish. It's important to have realistic expectations of your friendships so that you're not causing a problem out of something which isn't worthwhile.

Whilst it's normal to have the rose garden idea of friendship in your mind, it's important to keep your view realistic. Understand that life gets in the way sometimes and that people say and do hurtful things occasionally – just like you do from time to time too. Plans may be canceled for other things sometimes, misunderstandings happen, people prioritize other things over their friendships when they need to. A realistic view of a friendship bears all of this in mind and as a result, reduces the chances of a major problem occurring.

However, that doesn't mean you should allow your friends to constantly cancel your plans, and constantly take whatever you say the wrong way. In that case, it's not a friendship! It's about balance, and it's about understanding that sometimes in life, things go wrong and plans have to change. Don't take it to heart if a friend has to do this, just as they shouldn't take it to heart if you have to do so either.

In our next chapter I'm going to talk about how to handle conflicts in friendships but for now, let's focus on those expectations. That's the single best way to avoid a problem from happening in the first place.

Realistic Friendship Expectations

- Friends treat you with respect
- Friends do their best to avoid upsetting you or hurting your feelings
- You both make time for one another
- Your friendship doesn't push you or make you feel uncomfortable
- Friends make you laugh and make you feel better in general
- Friends support you when you're going through a hard time.

Unrealistic Friendship Expectations

- Close friendships bonds occur overnight
- You share your deepest secrets almost instantly
- You expect to spend a large amount of time together, even shortly after you meet
- You expect friends to drop everything and listen to you or be there for you at a moment's notice
- You expect to be their number one priority in life.

It's important to remember that real friendships have boundaries and they move at a pace that is comfortable for both people involved. Trust takes time to build up and by throwing your all into a friendship from the very first moment you meet, you're simply putting too much pressure on the potential friendship. If anything, you might also be scaring the other person away by being too much too soon. Slow down and allow the friendship to develop naturally, but remember to spend quality time together when you both can.

CHAPTER THOUGHTS

Friendships are wonderful things, but unlike what the movies tell you, they don't happen overnight, they're not going to fall into your lap, and you do need to put some effort in.

Having friends is important for your mental health and your general happiness, but you should also put in just as much as you take too. Remember to be there for your friends as much as they're there for you and always be present in the moment when you're spending time together.

It's also vital that you allow yourself to open up and be vulnerable at a pace that's comfortable to you. This doesn't mean sharing your darkest secrets and concerns if you're not comfortable doing so, but authentic relationships need vulnerability to help build trust. This can be difficult for people who have had difficult pasts and even for those who struggle with communication in general. Just go at a pace that's comfortable for you and don't feel rushed. You'll get there as long as you keep putting one foot in front of the other.

CONFLICTS ARISING AND HOW TO HANDLE THEM

As someone who struggled with shyness for a long time, I know how it feels when you start to make headway and you notice that you're connecting with people and making new friends. It's like you've got a new lease of life. It can also be terrifying because you're scared that you're going to say or do something to mess it up.

You have to relax into friendships and allow them to evolve. When a misunderstanding occurs, which it will at some point, do not panic! It's easy to go from 0 to 100 in less than a second and see disaster lights in front of your eyes but misunderstandings are easily cleaned up. Whilst learning how to improve your social skills and be a better communicator you have to know that mishaps are still going to happen, they're part of life. But, mishaps don't mean the end of friendships or opportunities, they're just a part of the story.

It's not possible to 'get' each other 100% of the time and there are always going to be occasions when you don't like something they did, or maybe they take offense to something you said or did. Part and parcel of friendship is accepting that people mess up sometimes and as long as work is done to repair it, i.e. an apology if one is necessary, these things can be overcome, swept under the rug, and forgotten. Maybe there is a lesson to be learned within that problem and in that case, certainly go ahead and learn it but don't assume that your newly formed friendship is over at the sign of the first hint of trouble.

In this chapter, I want to talk about conflicts within friendships and how you can handle them calmly and in the right way. Life sometimes throws us a few road bumps to keep us on our toes, but your new communication skills will help you out, even as they continue to grow and evolve.

NOT EVERYTHING CAN GO SMOOTHLY

If I've learned anything from life, it's that things rarely go as smoothly as you plan. Sometimes you have to take your hands off the control wheel and try and see where things go naturally. I've also learned that if something doesn't go as smoothly as you hoped, that's fine, because there will always be a way to steer it back on track, or maybe find another route that is even better than the one you had planned in the first place.

When you involve more than one person in a situation, there is a chance of misunderstanding and conflict. That's two individual people, two opinions, two egos, two sets of thoughts, two brains, and two lots of pride. Understand that people can be difficult! Friendships are littered with mishaps every so often but unless it's something earth-shatteringly bad that you've done, there is always an opportunity to fix it.

The information in this chapter will help you to deal with conflicts if and when they occur but having the right mindset from the start is important. Know that misunderstandings and problems happen in any friendship and that when they do happen, it's not the end of the world. Repeat that as a mantra as and when you need it!

CONFLICTS CAN BE BENEFICIAL

Believe it or not, conflicts can actually be very useful for a friendship. It's a little like a spring clean, it allows fresh air to enter the room, gets rid of the cobwebs, and leaves the scene feeling spick and span. A friendship that never experiences a difference of opinion, a misunderstanding, or a conflict in general probably isn't genuine or completely invested within. When emotions and opinions are involved, misunderstandings are bound to happen at some point, and it is even more confusing and even hurtful when it's a friend because this is someone you care about.

However, having the right mindset towards conflict means that you can look to solve the problem far easier and save some time. A relationship can grow and develop following a conflict, but it requires honesty and reflection to do that.

Of course, any type of conflict leaves you feeling upset and sad. It's confusing and you're not sure whether you feel guilty or attacked.

How you feel initially depends upon your view of conflict, which is developed throughout your early years. If you were taught to deal with issues constructively and to communicate clearly, you won't have as much trouble as someone who has always had problems with communication, i.e. you. However, the good news is that you can turn the tide on a conflict by understanding why they're actually quite useful. Two people who have had a conflict and a good conversation afterward can grow closer as a result.

Let's look at a few reasons why conflict can be useful.

Conflict gives you an opportunity to reflect

It could be that the conflict is designed to tell you something, i.e. your priorities are in the wrong place. Once you have a conflict, step back for a minute and look at the situation. What caused it? What can you learn from it? Did it happen because you aren't placing the right amount of interest in your friendship because you're not communicating clearly? Is the problem you're clashing over really worth it? Sometimes it's better to just allow things to pass and let things go.

Conflict identifies habits and behaviors that need to change

A conflict can be a sign that something needs to change, i.e. maybe you've developed a toxic habit or maybe your friend has. In that case, the conflict can serve as a wake-up call. If you're having regular arguments or misunderstandings, that makes it all the clearer that you need to look at things and assess what may need to change.

Don't see the conflict as a potential full stop to your friendship, instead see it as an opportunity to change things and breathe new life into a situation that is clearly struggling for some reason. Pay a little more attention to what you and also what your friend does and how you communicate with one another. This should give you the answers you seek.

Conflict serves as a learning curve

Any type of conflict gives you a chance to learn, especially when you look at what you're misunderstanding each other over, or what you're fighting about. That particular subject could be a trigger that needs to be resolved. Do you need to learn to be more understanding? Do you need to listen more? What is it that you can learn from the problem and what can you change in the future? Of course, this also means that your friend needs to do the same thing, in order for the learning opportunity to work.

COMMUNICATE WHEN YOU'RE UPSET

Much of the time, conflicts happen because of a communication problem. For instance, a misunderstanding happens because one person doesn't explain an issue clearly and the other person takes it to mean a different thing. Even a full-blown argument can be the fault of a problem with communication, because one person says something in a slightly off-hand or sarcastic way, and the other person takes offense to it.

Conflict, in its basic form, always comes down to communication issues.

This entire book is about learning to be a better communicator but sometimes that means taking it back a notch and using simple and clear language. You don't always have to be fancy or make everything complicated, sometimes the best approach is the simplest.

When you're upset about something, it can be easy to let your emotions get the better of you. For someone who doesn't have the highest level of EQ, this is quite likely to be the case. However, as you build up your EQ, become more confident in your ability to communicate, and as you develop your social skills, you'll be able to handle your own emotions, manage them, and stop them from causing you to act out in a way which could cause a conflict, or worsen an existing one.

When you try to resolve a conflict, the single best approach is a simple one. Simple and clear communication means that the other person knows how you feel, they understand what they did wrong, and they know how to stop it from happening again. Or, if you're at fault, simple and clear communication shows the other person that you know what you did, you understand it was wrong, and you're going to take steps to stop it from happening in the future. When you overcomplicate things, you run the risk of making the matter worse, even if your intentions are honorable.

The most likely emotion is anger and this is also one of the strongest too. Anger is responsible for almost every conflict if you look carefully at the root cause. Anger causes you to see red, it numbs you to the reality around you and it pushes you to say and do things that are extremely inadvisable.

Part of emotional intelligence is, of course, being in the moment and mindfully aware of what you're saying and doing. This is the single best technique when handling anger. Take a moment, stop and breathe, and count to ten. By taking yourself out of the situation for just a very small amount of time, you're able to gain perspective and that will stop you from doing anything that could come back to haunt you later on.

There are also some questions you should stop and ask yourself before you attempt to communicate with a person with who you are having a conflict with.

Question 1 – What do I want to get out of this?

Rather than reacting in the moment, stop and ask yourself what you want the outcome to be. In this situation, it's likely to be that you want to solve the conflict and for your friendship to be repaired. Keeping your aim in mind will stop you from saying or doing anything which could cause another outcome to occur, e.g. saying something in the heat of the moment in anger. By stopping and asking yourself this question, you're also giving yourself the time to calm down and gain perspective – that your friendship is worth more than this conflict.

Question 2 – What do I say to get the result I want?

Now you know what you want, it's time to think about the things you should say in order to get that result. That could be 'I'm sorry', or it could be 'I don't want us to argue', as a precursor to the conversation that hopefully solves the actual problem.

This time also allows you to think about how you say the word and not just the words themselves. You could say the most heartfelt sentence ever, but if you say it in the wrong way, perhaps with a hint of sarcasm and the wrong type of body language, it's going to amount to nothing and could even make the problem worse. Be heartfelt, open, and honest.

Remember to communicate your emotions to add authenticity, e.g. "I feel sad that we are fighting", or "I was angry".

Question 3 – How should I say it?

I just mentioned that you need to be mindful of your body language and you also need to avoid being sarcastic, because that totally takes away the meaning of your words and gives you the opposite effect. Before you actually go in and speak to your friend, work out how you're going to say it. Be mindful of the type of body language that is going to speak in your favor versus the type that is going to go against you.

Avoid crossing your arms over your body when you're speaking as that's classic defensive body language. This will tell the other person that you're not actually sorry and that you're feeling attacked. Instead, keep your arms down by your sides and maintain eye contact. The simplest body language is sometimes the best in these situations.

Speak slowly, carefully, and avoid any type of joke or sarcasm, even if it's meant to be humorous. It could be taken the wrong way and that will derail your efforts. Simple is best.

Question 4 – When should you speak to your friend?

To get the outcome you want, you need to choose your time carefully. Give yourself the time to calm down and be relaxed. Make sure you approach your friend at a time you know they're feeling calmer too and not when you know they're going to be in the middle of something important, e.g. picking up the kids from school or just finishing work.

You need to choose a time when you know that your efforts to smooth things over are going to be received well, rather than a time that is going to make it worse. You know your friend better than anyone, so give this some thought and don't feel rushed – a good communicator knows that there is no need to rush, the words and the sentiment will do the job when the time is right.

DO'S AND DON'TS OF HANDLING CONFLICT

When handling conflict, there are common do's and don'ts. Knowing these can stop you from going down the wrong route and potentially making things worse. When emotions are involved it's very easy to rush, but you need to calm down before you do anything. Make that your number one rule!

Do's of Handling Conflict

- **Choose your moment carefully** – As I mentioned in the last section, make sure that you choose your moment very carefully and wait until you're calm enough to speak without your emotions rising once more. You also need to choose a time when your friend is also going to have calmed down and a time which isn't going to be particularly bad for them in general.

- **Speak in person rather than via text if possible** – You can send a text to ask if you can meet up to talk, but have the actual conversation in person. Texts are so easy to misunderstand, and you could end up worsening the situation. Speaking in person also gives you the opportunity to read their body language and gain more from the meeting.

- **Keep things simple** – Simple communication is the best when calming a conflict. Don't say too much, don't overcomplicate it, don't use long-winded sentences that never really get to the point. Just keep it simple and say what you want to say.

- **Think about what you're going to say** – Whilst you can't rehearse a script because you don't know what the other person is going to say, you should think about what you want to say and what your aim of the conversation is. By doing so, you won't forget an important point and then kick yourself later on.

- **Be firm in your beliefs but keep your mind open too** – If you truly believe that what you said or did was right, or that you acted with the best intentions, but it went a little wrong, you can stick by your beliefs. You don't have to admit you were wrong if you weren't. Adults are able to agree to disagree. However, you should be open-minded enough to listen to their side of it and how they interpreted your words or actions and acknowledge that their view is just as valid as yours.

- **Use your breath to keep emotions under control** – If you feel like you're starting to become upset, turn your attention to your breath and bring your emotions under control. This is a very easy tactic you can use in many situations but when you're trying to communicate and you don't want your voice to wobble or your eyes to start watering, focus on something that isn't moving and turn your attention to your inhale and exhale. Make sure that you slow it down and stick to deep breaths. This will ground you and pull any rising emotions back into check.

- **Listen!** – It goes without saying that the number one do of dealing with conflict is that you should listen to your friend when they're speaking and show them that you are doing so. If you need a recap, go back to our chapter on listening and revisit the points we talked about. This is such an important aspect of handling conflict and could be the difference between a resolution and a further issue.

Don'ts of Handling Conflict

- **Be defensive, this isn't a battle** – If you did something wrong, admit it and move on. Do not allow yourself to become defensive and try and deflect the blame elsewhere. Also, avoid that defensive body language we talked about earlier. You are speaking to your friend here, not a fighter from an opposite army. Even when you're misunderstanding each other and conflicts are happening regularly, you're still friends and you still want the best for each other. There is no need to raise your walls and be defensive.

- **Drag up the conflict once more** – You're trying to solve the conflict, not continue it. Don't bring up points and start to argue once more. You can address points but, in a way, that means you're keen to move past them. By dragging up things that you don't agree with, you're just going to end up with round two.

- **Allow yourself to become emotional** – In the 'do' section we talked about using your breath to bring your emotions under control and that is very important. By becoming emotional, you're going to potentially say something you regret and not really get the outcome you want. Stay as balanced as you can possibly be and focus on resolution.

- **Say too much** – There's no need to give a big speech. When you're thinking about what you're going to say, keep it as simple as possible. This gives you less chance of being misunderstood and more chance of your friend being on the same page as you.

- **Make it all about you** – It takes two people to make a friendship and two people to start and continue an argument. When trying to resolve it, that means it's not all about you either. Respect the other person's point of view and whilst it's very easy to get wrapped up in how it feels to you and how it hurt you, remember that it probably hurt your friend also. Keep it balanced and appreciate both sides.

DEALING WITH SOMEONE DIFFICULT

As you start to branch out into meeting new people, it's inevitable that you'll meet one or two which test your patience. There are some difficult people out there and whilst we should always give the benefit of the doubt and give everyone a chance, some people are just beyond it!

Difficult people can be thrown into your path in any situation. You might meet someone at the bus stop who just will not stop complaining, you might have to deal with an angry customer at work, or you might befriend someone who seemed great initially but then began to completely rely upon you for emotional support 24 hours a day. It's worth remembering that someone could be just having a bad day but if you experience difficult behavior from the same person on a few occasions, you have to stop and think about whether you really need this in your life.

Let's look at a few examples of difficult people you might encounter and why they're so hard to deal with.

- **Mood Vacuums** – These types of people literally suck the life out of you because they're always so negative and rarely have anything good to say. This type of person can never be pleased and they're often complaining or dragging others down. In the end, you'll feel just as negative and your mood will plummet!
- **Show Offs** – These people always have to go one better and be the best in the room. If you have a new iPhone, they'll

have the brand-new version. If you're feeling good, they're feeling amazing. They do this to some degree because they need the validation to feel good, but the constant comparisons and trying to be better than everyone else is nothing but exhausting.

- **Bossy Types** – The bossy people are often the worst to deal with because they're never wrong (so they think) and they're not going to think twice at stamping over you to get what they want. The best advice with this type of person is to just let them do what they do and walk away. You'll never change them.

- **Doormats** – This type of person is the type you want to grab and shake, try to get some life or emotion out of them. They don't say or do much, they often let other people do their unfair share of work, and they'll just agree to everything you say. Annoying, to say the least.

- **Manipulators** – These people are dangerous, and they're often dressed up as someone you can trust and someone you might like but they end up being worse than the bossy types and can manipulate you into saying or doing anything they want. This category also includes narcissists and it's best to try and avoid them at all costs.

If you feel exhausting dealing with someone on a regular basis and they just don't make you feel good no matter what you try and do, it's probably a very clear sign that this person isn't meant to be in your social circle. If this is someone at work, you're going to just have to tolerate them for your working hours as best you can, perhaps holding them at arm's length. For everyone else, deal with them when you have to and stay the hell away for the rest of the time!

Aside from the types of people you're likely to meet, it's important to know a few techniques you can use to handle these people when they're in front of you. Let's look at that now.

Set boundaries and time limits

If someone makes you feel negative or simply causes you to roll your eyes on a constant basis, you need to set time limits for how long you're going to stay around them and boundaries for what you will and won't tolerate. This is the only way to come out of the situation relatively unscathed and to save your sanity.

For instance, if you have a colleague at work who is always complaining and very negative, you can't just walk away from them because you have to work alongside them and it's rude. However, you can set time limits and boundaries as to how much you'll tolerate before you walk away. You could listen to them for five minutes in the morning around the coffee machine and then make your excuses to leave and go about your day.

Be mindful of your emotions

If someone is really making you feel down and negative, you have the right to walk away from them, politely of course. You need to be aware of your emotions and be mindful of how someone makes you feel. Never ignore your gut, especially when it comes to people and the vibe they give to you.

Smother them in kindness

No matter what type of person you're dealing with, you can't go wrong if you approach the situation with total kindness and compassion. They might hate it secretly, but at least you're doing the right thing! By using this tactic, you're ridding yourself of any bad karma and you're deflecting their negative traits back at them.

Search for some common ground

It's likely that you don't really want to be friends with this type of person, but you still need to have a rapport with the amount of time you need to spend with them. Remember, the best way to build a rapport? By looking for common ground. You might have to search hard and be creative, but there will always be something you can use to build a conversation and steer it away from negativity.

Stay calm

I mentioned being aware of your emotions but if you're dealing with someone who is quite angry and irate, it's vital that you stay calm. If you're dealing with a manipulator, again, stay calm and don't allow them to get into your head. By focusing on your breath, you can keep your own anger in check and your emotions still.

Focus on what you can control

Some people cannot be changed, and you shouldn't ever try. However, you can focus on the things you can control and forget about the rest. For instance, if you're at work and you're dealing with an irate customer, focus on finding a solution and forget the rest. If you're dealing with a friend who is expecting you to be at their beck and call 24 hours a day, set the boundaries we talked about earlier and focus on controlling your emotions and your response. You don't have to answer all the time, not if the person is invading your personal time with family and not being respectful.

CHAPTER THOUGHTS

Most people do not like conflict, myself included. However, conflict is an essential part of life because it allows us to learn and grow. The key is to address conflict in the right and timely manner and to stop problems from festering and becoming infected.

When you have your first conflict with a friend, it's possible that you'll panic and think that the friendship is doomed. It's not. Conflict can be healthy and can help you to become closer over time. All you need to do is be aware of the do's and don'ts that allow you to overcome conflict without making things worse.

As you become more confident in your new social skills, you'll also open yourself up to the chance of more conflict, simply because you're dealing with other people on a regular basis. See this as a positive development in your journey and approach every misunderstanding and conflict as an opportunity to learn more.

DEEPENING CURRENT RELATIONSHIPS IN YOUR LIFE

So far, we've talked about using your social skills to meet new people, build a rapport, and then deepen a connection to the point where it may lead to a friendship. At the start of this book you probably never thought that you would be able to do that.

During my earlier years, my shyness held me back from speaking to anyone in this way. If you'd told me back then that I'd be sitting here writing a book, helping others overcome the same thing in the way I have, I'd have laughed at you! However, take my success as motivation and a testimonial into how this whole process can completely revolutionize your life, not just your social skills.

There is one last thing you need to be mindful of – that you don't become so excited about meeting new people and creating new connections that you forget about the ones you already have in your life.

FRIENDSHIPS IN ADULTHOOD

In childhood, friendship is easy. You can bond over the cute color of your sweater and you'll be playing in the sandpit for hours afterward. However, as adulthood takes over, it becomes harder than ever to find the time to dedicate to our friendships. As we've already talked about, one of the most important aspects of any friendship is spending quality time together.

In many ways, this issue is that life becomes busy and takes us in different directions. Friends go traveling, maybe they move to another country, some get married, maybe they have children, and others become so engrossed in their career that they don't have much time for anything else. As we move through life, we also meet a new group of people and it's very easy to feel closer to them because they're reflecting the state of our life right now. Our childhood friends, or the friends we made earlier in our lives, might not provide you with the same common ground anymore.

However, it's important to remember that common ground rarely changes that much, and the longer you've been friends with someone, the more important it is to keep that friendship alive.

Let's look at a few ways you can make time to catch up with your friends, even in today's busy, modern world.

Create a group WhatsApp chat – Even if you don't have the time to catch up regularly, you can do so virtually via messaging apps. If you have a group of childhood friends or friends you've known for a while, create a WhatsApp group and you can stay in touch with each other on a very regular basis, without much trouble whatsoever.

Connect on social media – If you don't want to set up messaging apps, you can simply connect on social media and stay up to date with what the other one is doing. However, do be mindful that your connection should not be simply virtual and that you do need to meet up in person to keep the friendship alive.

Have a day every month/week you arrange to do something – Everyone can spare one day or evening a month, surely! If you can stretch this to a week, try it but if not once every fortnight or once every month for a catch-up is a great idea. You could go out for a meal and some drinks or simply go out for a coffee and a good chat in the afternoon, but do not cancel it!

Make your time together a priority – Maintaining long-term friendships is about making them a priority and not letting life take over. The moment you start to cancel and rearrange meetings, take it as a warning to be more mindful of what you're doing. It's a slippery slope towards growing apart and that's not something you want.

STAYING IN TOUCH

I've already talked about the fact that as we move through life, it simply becomes busier. It's easy to turn all your attention to the new things in your life and before you know it, you're forgetting about everything that was there before, old friends included. Staying in touch isn't difficult, and it takes literally a few seconds to send a quick "I hope you're okay" text.

Start to view staying in touch as less of a burden and more of a positive habit you get into on a regular basis. You probably call home to your parents every week, so why not do the same with your older friends?

A busy life shouldn't stop you from staying in touch with people and failure to do so actually points towards a lack of interest, more than a busy life. Nurturing relationships comes down to keeping the connection alive and even if you can't stop everything and meet up for coffee, you can do a small thing that shows your friend that you're thinking of them and that they're important in your life.

A few ideas include:

- Stopping by for a coffee on your way home from work
- Sending a text to check in with them and see how they are
- Remembering birthdays, anniversaries, children's birthdays, etc.
- Sending funny memes and gifs via WhatsApp, just because
- Tagging friends in things you see on Facebook and commenting "do you remember when … "
- Asking if they have time for a coffee during your lunch break at work.

As you can see, it doesn't have to take a long time, it doesn't even have to be something huge, it's just a point of keeping the connection burning and allowing the friendship to be nurtured over the long-term, no matter how busy life gets.

THE LITTLE THINGS MATTER

Sometimes it's the small things in life which mean the most, don't you agree? It really is the thought that counts more than the grand gestures in life and when it comes to keeping a friendship alive during adulthood, this whole concept is bang on the money.

The knowledge that is needed, you'd be there for your friend is far more comforting and valuable than a huge bunch of flowers. A text at exactly the right time can brighten your day and put a smile on your face more than anything else. A cheeky smile when you both 'get' an in-joke can make you feel completely uplifted. None of these things are huge gestures but they're extremely valuable.

Of course, it would be nice if you had an old friend who regularly sent you huge gifts and offered to whisk you away on a vacation occasionally but what does that even mean? Gifts are pleasant but they don't have the same deep connection beneath them that thought does. A text saying "I know today is the anniversary of your mother's passing. I just wanted to send my love and know that I'm thinking of you". That text on a day like that could be the difference between that person choosing to drown their sorrows in wine when they get home or be able to face the day with some amount of strength. That's the power of friendship.

If you have an old friend who works in the opposite office to you and you simply don't have much time to catch up these days, buying her a coffee and leaving it on her desk as you walk by, with a cheeky smile, is enough to make her feel ten times better. It's about noticing when someone isn't feeling good, it's about remembering special days, and it's just about showing that you're willing to keep putting in the effort.

Small things matter.

BE OPEN TO CHANGE

Friendships change. This is something I've learned a lot over the years. This situation is especially pertinent when you have friends from childhood. My closest friend is someone I've known since I was 2 years old. Our friendship has endured 36 years and counting, through the deaths of both her parents, my moving away, teenage arguments, and ultimately her getting married. That was the biggest change for me because it meant she was in a completely different space in her life compared to me.

At first, I was a little worried about it, because how would it change your friendship? It did change it, but has it changed for the worse? No. Change doesn't have to be bad, and you have to be open to it and embrace it if you want to keep important friendships in your life. You can't force people to stay in the same space their entire lives, it's just not possible, just like you can't be forced to do the same either. What you need to do is adjust and adapt, knowing that if your friendship is strong enough, you've got a great chance at keeping it alive.

Friendships change during adulthood naturally, simply because *we* change. Throughout your life, you might be deeply rooted as the same person, but different facets of your personality and your inner psyche are always shifting and changing. When I was trapped in a cycle of shyness, I was a very unconfident and quiet person, however now I'm entirely different. Am I a different person underneath? No, but the way I do things has changed. That's why friendships change.

Dealing with change is hard for anyone but it's important to see it as a positive thing and not a negative. If you're noticing that your friendships are changing, here are a few tips to help you cope with the overall change.

- **Give things time to settle** – When a change occurs, it's likely to need a little time for the ground to settle. Don't be worried about that and in the meantime, stay in touch with text messages and small touches here and there.
- **Change your viewpoint** – Try to see things from their side and understand that maybe they're going through a stressful time in life, or maybe they're so excited about the big change in their life that they're seeing things through tunnel vision right now. Use your empathy to deal with the moment.
- **Talk it through** – Talk about your feelings with a trusted friend and seek their advice. Often, allowing ourselves to listen to another person's view helps us to reframe the situation more positively.
- **Focus on yourself in the meantime (but don't forget them)** – Whilst the ground is settling focus on yourself and head out to meet new people. That doesn't

mean you're forgetting about your friend, but you're simply giving them the time they need to adjust to their new change.

It can be hard when friendships change but hanging onto the past and wanting things to remain the same is just going to bring you sadness in the end. It's far better to be willing to go with the flow and allow friendships to evolve. Most of the time, you end up with something far more valuable than you began with – a friendship that has endured.

Of course, there may be times when a friendship doesn't endure, when the other person drifts too far away and they don't put in their necessary side of the effort. This is a very hard thing to handle and it can be extremely upsetting, but you must see this as something which is inevitable in life and something you can overcome.

I've had friends come and go and many have left my life because we've just drifted. This wasn't anyone's fault, and it wasn't down to a lack of effort, it's just one of those things. When a friend leaves your life, wish them well, send them love, and focus on the good memories you have. If you allow yourself to become bitter about the fact that your friendship drifted away, you're just going to affect how you interact with people in the future.

In this case, simply hold your current friendships that little bit closer and know that life has an odd way of righting itself in the end.

IT'S THE QUALITY FOR ME

We live in a world dominated by social media. We're all obsessed with getting x number of likes and hitting a certain number of friends. But, do you count these people as real friends? I don't.

For me, I have social media friends, who I would prefer to call followers, and I have real friends. Some of my real friends are also on my social media but it's the time we spend away from our phones and laptops that is most important.

As you build up your social skills, you're probably going to do your best to find as many new friends as possible. You're flexing your new communication muscles and I can't blame you for it – you deserve a huge pat on the back. However, know that in the end, it's quality over quantity that really matters.

How many of your friends would be there if you really needed them? Those are the ones you need to focus on the most. It's nice to have a lot of friends, for sure, but the ones who would be there for you are the ones that are the most precious and count the most.

I would recommend doing a social media inventory every so often. Not everyone on that list may be serving you well. As you strive to hit a certain number of followers or "friends", you might be adding people who using your social media accounts as a surveillance tool, rather than because they're genuinely interested in what you're up to in your life. Toxic friends aren't friends, they're just people you really don't need in your life.

If anyone makes you feel uncomfortable, takes far more than they give, talks behind your back, manipulates you, belittles you, or spreads false rumors about you, delete them and move on. This should be no detriment to you because these people are not real friends. I've lost count of the number of people I thought were my friends only to turn out to be toxic individuals who had another agenda. Don't give them another second of your time and delete them from your life, virtually and realistically.

I'm not suggesting you go having a friendship cull every six months, but just be aware that having real friends you can rely upon is far more important than having a long list of people who might appear to be your friends, but are actually far from it. Quality is far more important!

CHAPTER THOUGHTS

Friendships come and go, but the best ones endure over the long-term. Maintaining friendships into adulthood is hard and nobody should ever try to tell you any differently. My closest friend and I lost touch for a short amount of time in our early 20s and came back together again around 5 years later. We're closer than we've ever been because we learned from our mistakes and we put in the effort to stay in touch, even though there's currently quite a lot of actual distance between us.

It's great to have a lot of friends and when you start flexing your social skills, you'll find that you meet people far more easily than you ever did before. However, within that, make sure you remember your old friends and make time for them. Loyalty counts for a lot and that's what will show you who the real ones are versus the ones who will come into your life, stay for a while, and then drift back out again.

Know that not everyone is meant to stay in your life and as painful as it can be sometimes, you have to allow the flow to do its thing. People often drift apart and there's nothing to pull them back, but you should always try to make that connection once more before you give up.

As friendships change, know that you're changing too and not all of it is bad.

CONCLUSION

And there we have it!

We've reached the end of the book. How do you feel now? I hope you're feeling confident, invigorated, and that you're looking forward to the countless opportunities that are sitting right in front of you.

Maybe you have started on your journey towards communication mastery already, or maybe you have read the book cover to cover before making a start. Whatever route you have taken, know that the next steps are in your hands. Your future does not have to look like the past. You don't have to let barriers stand in your way of having the life you want, and you can change anything you want to change, as long as you put in the work.

Your social skills are a million times more important than you know. They affect every single thing in your life, from how you make friends to how you maintain them, how you find work that fulfills you, to how you learn and grow. They affect how you see yourself and how you interact with others, and they affect how you read people. Social skills also affect how you manage your emotions, because they link so closely to emotional intelligence.

By reading this book and taking the advice I've given you, your emotional intelligence level will rise. It's inevitable because as you take the steps outlined throughout the book, you're improving your social skills, you're becoming a far better communicator, and you're learning about people every single day. I hope you feel excited right now because I feel excited for you. Oh, the possibilities!

Right now, I want you to imagine the life you want for yourself. Go on, allow yourself to dream for a minute. What does it look like? What does it feel like? Are you smiling? You should be, because that image you have in your mind right now could be your life in a relatively short amount of time. You might not believe me completely right now but ask anyone who knew me before I made my own journey.

I was a shy and very quiet person. It's not that I was introverted and it's not that I wasn't confident in myself – I was, I just wasn't confident in speaking to other people and that affected every single part of my life detrimentally. You see, once you make a decision to change something and you really go for it, there is no stopping you. And once that confidence takes hold and you know that you can do the one thing you didn't believe you could ever do before, it's a feeling like no other.

YOUR JOURNEY STARTS WITH ONE STEP

All you need to do is decide to change and do it. It sounds like a huge undertaking but that's because you've built it up in your mind to be that. It's not. It's just small exercises every day that will snowball into this massive change in your life.

We started the book by talking about emotional intelligence (EQ) and what it is. Your level is pretty low right now because you've openly admitted to having low social skills by picking up this book, but that's going to change quite rapidly!

We've talked about what social skills are and why they're important, and you now know that in every aspect of your life, your ability to communicate in the right way makes a huge difference. I've given you plenty of practice help and advice on how to get started, including where you can go to meet new friends. The onus really is on you to do all of this but know that at any point you can go back to this book and find someone who understands you. I do. I get all of this because I was there. I believe in you.

We've talked about the things you might be doing to sabotage your efforts to meet new people and you know exactly what you need to do to make changes. You know everything there is to know about first impressions, body language, non-verbal communication, and how to get your message across and make sure that you're understood.

We finished up the book by talking in detail about friendships and how to handle the trials and tribulations that come alongside them. Whilst friendships take work and they certainly come with a fair amount of drama attached to them occasionally, they are one of the most valuable things you'll ever have in your life. Supportive, genuine, and caring friends will help you through the hardest times and share your joy in the good times. That's exactly what you have to look forward to.

SO, NOW WHAT?

Now the time has come for you to take everything you've learned in this book and put it into firm action. Work in a way that suits you best. Maybe you've started already, but if not, you can start chapter by chapter and work slowly if you want, or you can read all the way through, make notes, and then get to work. Everyone learns in a different way so make sure that you tailor your approach to your own learning needs.

If you forget something or you need clarification, you can simply go back to the chapter you need and find the answers. This book will always be by your side throughout your journey and beyond. You might think that this journey has an end date – it doesn't. My journey still hasn't finished I'm still learning. People are very complicated begins and we have to grow and adjust depending upon the people who come into our lives and their particular personalities. We're constantly kept on our toes and that's what makes it so wonderful!

Start small or start big, work in your own way. However, if you're someone who struggles with social anxiety or shyness, work slowly and know that every small win you have along the way is huge progress. This isn't a race and nobody else even has to know what you're trying to do – the results will become very evident to them when your confidence levels are transformed and you begin to carry yourself naturally in a way that makes you glow from the inside, out.

You might have the odd mishap along the way and know that's normal. You might wake up one day and feel completely off your game. That doesn't mean all the progress you've made so far has gone to waste, it just means that you're having a bad day and you need to be kind to yourself. We all have those days, we're human after all.

All that's left for me to do now is to wish you good luck. The power to change your life is in your hands and you and you alone can make the changes you really want to see. Remember to pat yourself on the back and celebrate every success, whilst also helping other people around you who may need some help with their social skills. Share the knowledge and let's build people up!

Your journey has only just begun.

REFERENCES

A New Layered Model on Emotional Intelligence. (2018, May 1). PubMed Central (PMC). https://www.ncbi.nlm.nih.gov/pmc/articles/PMC5981239/

Advances in the Research of Social Anxiety and Its Disorder (Special Section). (n.d.). PubMed Central (PMC). https://www.ncbi.nlm.nih.gov/pmc/articles/PMC2846378/

Behavioral inhibition system and self-esteem as mediators between shyness and social anxiety. (2018, December 1). ScienceDirect. https://www.sciencedirect.com/science/article/abs/pii/S0165178117323326

Body language in the brain: constructing meaning from expressive movement. (2015). PubMed Central (PMC). https://www.ncbi.nlm.nih.gov/pmc/articles/PMC4543892/

Everything You Ever Wanted to Know About Shyness in an International Context. (n.d.). American Psychological Association. https://www.apa.org/international/pi/2017/06/shyness

Gibbons, S. (2018, June 20). *You And Your Business Have 7 Seconds To Make A First Impression: Here's How To Succeed.* Forbes. https://www.forbes.com/sites/serenitygibbons/2018/06/19/you-have-7-seconds-to-make-a-first-impression-heres-how-to-succeed/?sh=1897dbf656c2

O'Connor, P. J. (2019). *The Measurement of Emotional Intelligence: A Critical Review of the Literature and Recommendations for Researchers and Practitioners.* Frontiers. https://www.frontiersin.org/articles/10.3389/fpsyg.2019.01116/full

Okten, I. O. (2018, January 31). *Studying First Impressions: What to Consider?* Association for Psychological Science - APS. https://www.psychologicalscience.org/observer/studying-first-impressions-what-to-consider

Social relations and life satisfaction: the role of friends. (2018). PubMed Central (PMC). https://www.ncbi.nlm.nih.gov/pmc/articles/PMC5937874/

Speaking of Psychology: Nonverbal Communication Speaks Volumes. (n.d.). American Psychological Association. https://www.apa.org/research/action/speaking-of-psychology/nonverbal-communication

Tadjer, H., Lafifi, Y., Derindere, M., Gulsecen, S., & Seridi-Bouchelaghem, H. (2018, September 13). *What Are The Important*

Social Skills of Students in Higher Education? ResearchGate. https://www.researchgate.net/ publication/329761072_What_Are_The_Important_Social_Skills_of_ Students_in_Higher_Education

www.ingramcontent.com/pod-product-compliance
Lightning Source LLC
Chambersburg PA
CBHW030245030426
42336CB00009B/260